Beautiful Knitting:

Techniques and Patterns
for Creating Elegant Designs

By Luce Smits

Photography by
Jean-Charles Vaillan

Translation by
Kim M. Allen Gleed

Sterling Publishing Co., Inc.

New York

Translated from the French by Kim M. Allen Gleed

Library of Congress Cataloging-in-Publication Data

Smits, Luce.

  Beautiful knitting : techniques and patterns for creating elegant designs / Luce Smits.

    p. cm.

  Includes index.

  ISBN-13: 978-1-4027-2631-6

  ISBN-10: 1-4027-2631-7

  1. Knitting—Patterns. I. Title.

TT820.S5446 2006

746.43'2—dc22

                                                2006005292

10 9 8 7 6 5 4 3 2 1

Published in 2006 by Sterling Publishing Co., Inc.

387 Park Avenue South, New York, NY 10016

Published originally under the title *Le tricot: techniques et modèles*

© 2004 by Editions Solar, Paris

English translation copyright © 2006 by Sterling Publishing Co., Inc.

Distributed in Canada by Sterling Publishing

c/o Canadian Manda Group, 165 Dufferin Street

Toronto, Ontario, Canada M6K 3H6

Distributed in the United Kingdom by GMC Distribution Services

Castle Place, 166 High Street, Lewes, East Sussex, England BN7 1XU

Distributed in Australia by Capricorn Link (Australia) Pty. Ltd.

P.O. Box 704, Windsor, NSW 2756, Australia

Sterling ISBN-13: 978-1-4027-2631-6

      ISBN-10: 1-4027-2631-7

For information about custom editions, special sales, premium and

corporate purchases, please contact Sterling Special Sales

Department at 800-805-5489 or specialsales@sterlingpub.com.

For Louise

Contents

Introduction

The hand does what the heart requests.
Zhuang-zi

I have never stopped knitting; I have always loved it.

Over the years, I have had the pleasure of sharing my passion and my professional skill with experimental knitters who have become friends. I have met increasing numbers of young women who want to learn to knit, to find a bit of themselves in an age-old craft; perhaps also to slip away for a moment, between classes at university, while traveling, when they are under pressure, or on vacation.

Tackling a simple stitch and, later, learning to vary it to make the season's latest accessory, becomes a necessity. Confidence has been established, and the technical roadblocks have been overcome. You progress, step by step, modestly at first, but then, with all the joy of a creator—like an architect or a builder—you see the project take shape, an original idea that you will be proud to wear.

Beginning knitting means:

- taking time, placing yourself in this low-key world, becoming refocused on the essence of your own accomplishment;
- progressing, in pursuit of perfection, toward a real place, offering yourself a single present, born of a first movement, that which formed the world;
- placing yourself at the point of encountering one of the oldest crafts, the long known techniques, the diverse cultures and places, feeling the growing desire to distinguish yourself in a world where orthodoxy and uniformity have lost their appeal.

The relationship of the craft to the environment renewed, the simplicity of the tools, the apprenticeship and the bond between you, the knitter, and the materials incites a constant creation, a step by step journey where an ancient domestic art becomes an unexpected pleasure, a creative process, an amazing luxury, or even a job. Unlike industrialization, which tends to homogenize everything, and mechanical crafts, with their ever more rapid rhythms to condition us, knitting returns to its rightful place of importance once more in the limelight.

I simply wish, by way of this book, to attract newcomers, to persuade beginners that right now or tomorrow they can acquire, patiently, with their own hands, a mastery that they in turn will be able to pass on. As for already confirmed artists, I hope they will consider this work as a simple tool, a daily companion!

Luce Smits

Short History

From the most ancient times, knitting has been an integral part of the production of textiles: stitches, techniques, the use of colors has evolved alongside cultures, to the rhythm of civilizations. While we may have lost, over the centuries, the symbolic meaning of certain stitches and certain uses, knitting still remains an essential element in our heritage.

Ten centuries before Jesus Christ, nomadic people from Arabia wore sandal socks knitted by hand, and across the world knitted clothing was in use in the ancient civilizations in Peru. At the beginning of our common era, the Old English word cnytte, meaning "to knit" began appearing in the Oxford dictionary.

In later centuries, knitting spread west from the Orient with the Arab conquests and found a home in Europe, via Spain. The introduction of silk from China helped knitting to evolve toward very sophisticated forms, and silk stockings, from Mantua, Italy, spread throughout Europe at the beginning of the Renaissance. Then France became a very busy center: guilds specialized in knitting silk stockings and exported them widely. Silver and gold thread also arrived from China, and these threads were used to embellish the silk. They were quickly followed by pearls and embroidery, which further decorated the pieces.

In the sixteenth century, the defeat of the Spanish Armada, whose ships ran aground on the coasts of England and Scotland, brought, thanks to the captured sailors, new knitting textures with raised designs.

Different regions in Europe are distinguished by their specialties: lace stitches (France, Holland, the Shetland Islands), textures with raised, embroidered patterns (Austria, central Europe), simple, thick pullover sweaters made of natural rustic wool (Denmark, Iceland), cable designs (Ireland, Iran), nautical stitches and oiled wools for time spent at sea . . .

1850: invention of the first knitting machine by the Englishman William Lee

1900: industrialization of the profession

1980: explosion of hand-made knitting in western Europe; wider variety of threads became available

1990: opening of international markets, bringing a massive relocation of knitting factories to lower-salary countries; installation of large Japanese-type industrial machines which create knitting that looks handmade in the factories.

2000: renewed interest in the world of knitting, past-times, fashion, and decoration. Changing patterns of work and leisure allow for more creativity.

1

Materials and Tools

The Yarns

The yarns, along with the needles, are the basic elements of all knitting. The choice of threads is very important because it determines the stitches to use, the success of the pattern, and the final appearance of the overall work. The most commonly used yarns are classified according to their origin: animal, vegetable, or synthetic.

YARNS OF ANIMAL ORIGIN

Yarns of animal origin are the most numerous on the market. The best known, longest used, and most widely used yarn in knitting is wool.

Wool

This yarn comes from different species of sheep. There are many types of wool.

Regional wool. It is produced on every continent where sheep live. It is worked as easily in knitting as it is in weaving: shepherds' sweaters, nomadic carpets, tents to live in. . . . It is characterized by its rustic appearance and great durability.

Shetland wool. Originating in the Shetland Islands off Scotland, this native wool is very fine and is oiled before being spun to keep it strong and flexible during the process. After spinning the oil is washed out. The colors can also be plied to create tweeds and marls. This wool is sold in small skeins. It is also made into beautiful woven fabrics, known as *Harris Tweed.*

Lamb's wool. This very soft wool is obtained from the first shearing of lambs, aged 6 to 7 months. Fine and supple, it is perfect to blend with luxury yarns such as cashmere, angora, or

The natural beauty of regional wool

The subtlety of tweeds and marled yarns

camel hair, making them stronger and reducing their cost.

Merino wool. Fine, soft, and very smooth with particularly long fibers, it comes from merino sheep raised mainly in Australia and New Zealand.

Mohair and Kid Mohair

These two yarns come from angora goats that originally came from Pakistan. From their very long curly hair, you obtain soft, warm, and lightweight knitting yarns. Young goats give us kid mohair.

Mohair and kid mohair should be knitted with simple stitches so that the beauty of the yarn is highlighted. To obtain a fuller effect, there are small mohair brushes designed to fluff the hair after knitting.

Angora

This is obtained by plucking the fur of the angora rabbit. (The rabbit is not hurt.) The threads are fine, light, and very absorbent; because of their fragility, they are most often blended with lamb's wool. Clothes and accessories made of angora have a unique feel, thanks to the extreme softness of the material. The fur of the angora rabbit may be plucked several times a year.

Cashmere

This yarn comes to us from Asia. In the Himalayas live goats who possess one of the softest and most silky coats in the animal kingdom; the hairs are collected by combing, once a year, and each animal provides less than 4 ounces (100 g) at each combing!

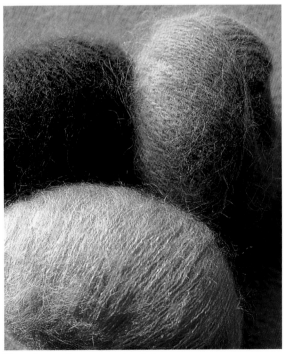

The softness of angoras and mohairs

Given the scarcity and the market value of this yarn, tufts of hair caught on thorny bushes, tree branches, and on the wire screens over which the goats have brushed are carefully collected as well.

Finally (also taking into account its cost), cashmere yarn is often blended with lamb's wool, merino wool, or silk.

Camel Hair

Camel hair is used in its natural state, undyed. It is most often blended with merino wool which allows for a variation in color. Shiny and durable, today it is most frequently used to make luxurious woven fabrics.

Alpaca

Its name is taken from the animal in the camel family living in the high plateaus of the Andes mountains, nearly three miles (5,000 m) high. This yarn, with its unique thermal properties, is very durable and very beautiful. It is used undyed because it is available in a wide variety of natural colors.

Silk

It was brought into the West in the first centuries of our common era via the long commercial route called the Silk Road which stretched from China

NOTE

The worms must eat 90 plus pounds (45 kg) of mulberry leaves to produce, during their metamorphosis, about 15 pounds (7 kg) of cocoon, from which is drawn less than 18 ounces (500 g) of silk. The work of unwinding the cocoons to convert them into raw yarn is done by hand.

to Rome. Natural silk comes from the silk worm (the bombyx), which is nourished by the leaves of the white mulberry bush. Today, it is mainly produced in China and India, although in France (especially in the Cévennes region, which has for many years cultivated the silk worm), there are

The rustic nature of raw silk

The shimmer of dyed silks

still some silk worm breeders (called sericulturists) who provide their product for artisans. The silk obtained has a shiny appearance and possesses, among other traits, a great capacity for insulation: worn in winter, a silk garment is warm; in summer, it is cool. The great durability of silk gives it many uses. Silk should be knitted with a firm tension.

YARNS OF VEGETABLE ORIGIN

Among the most well-known threads in this family are cotton, linen, hemp, jute, raffia, and ramie. The most commonly used fibers in knitting are cotton, known since antiquity, and linen. These threads may be blended with viscose (pure, chemically treated cellulose), wool, and/or synthetic fibers.

Cotton

This widely known vegetable fiber is one of the oldest yarns used in knitting and weaving. Cotton is a plant that grows in tropical and subtropical regions. It has a great capacity for water absorption and it is very durable. Available in the United States, one of the principal worldwide producers is a genetically grown, already-tinted cotton. The shades are soft and natural looking.

Cotton begins as a soft matte fiber, but it can be treated to make it stronger and much more lustrous. This process is called mercerizing. Cotton perfectly adapts to summer knits and is hypoallergenic. It may be blended with linen, wool, or synthetics.

Strength and beauty in a range of cottons

The sophistication of linen yarns

Linen

An elegant yarn from the stem of the flax plant, linen has been worked for nearly five thousand years and has been used in the west since the Middle Ages.

Today, cultivated linen from the European Union (Belgium, Italy, Ireland, France, Austria, Spain, Portugal) bears the label "Linen Masters/Maîtres du lin," which is the sign of its superior quality. It has a shiny appearance and is dry to the touch. It is knitted as is or blended with cotton, viscose, or silk.

Ramie, Hemp, Raffia, Jute

Also of vegetable origin, these yarns are most often used for weaving.

SYNTHETIC YARNS

Synthetic yarns, which are often blended with natural fibers to make the natural fibers less expensive and more easily machine washable, come in many different types. They are most often derived from petroleum, and their chemical composition allows the manufacturer to create a broad spectrum of beautiful yarns that are as useful for knitting as they are for weaving.

One thinks of acrylic yarns, polyamides, polyesters, lamés, metallics, and lurex, which are widely used in today's hand knitting. All of these yarns, like natural yarns, can be combed, looped, or curled to give many beautiful effects. Chenille yarns, for example, present the effect and softness of velour.

The Japanese have recently begun selling paper-based yarns which are ribbon-like and can be worked as other fibers. Research on these plant-based fabrics shows that they have the ability to filter ultraviolet rays.

Fibers can be blended to create many different types of yarns

Ribbons and intertwined strands in matte and shiny finish

The Tools

Needles constitute the most simple and the most common tools of all: they are compact and inexpensive, and are easy to use and transport. What is more practical? Other accessories accompany them in order to facilitate the progression of your knitting during the different steps of the process.

NEEDLES

Needles come in all sorts of sizes, lengths, and types.

Single-Pointed Needles

Made of metal, bamboo, or wood, one end is pointed and the other has a stopper, which prevents the stitches from dropping in the course of the work. Most needles have their size noted either on the stopper or on the needle itself. These needles are used in pairs, and their length varies: the most commonly used are those measuring either 10 or 14 inches (30 or 40 cm).

You can find needles made of plastic, glass, and even whale bone (baleen) should you decide to search.

Double-Pointed Needles

Often called "sock needles," these are generally available in 7- or 10-inch lengths and in the same materials as single-pointed needles. They are sold in sets of four or five. You evenly distribute, or as the pattern instructs you, the stitches over three or four needles, and you use the fourth or the fifth to knit. This system allows you to knit circular pieces such as gloves, socks, or legwarmers.

Circular Needles

These often replace straight needles. They are composed of two rigid pointed ends joined by a flexible cord, and come in many sizes and lengths. They allow you to work in the round or

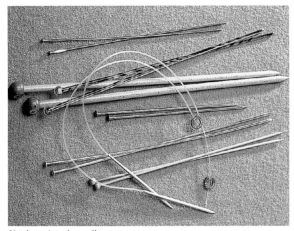

Single-pointed needles

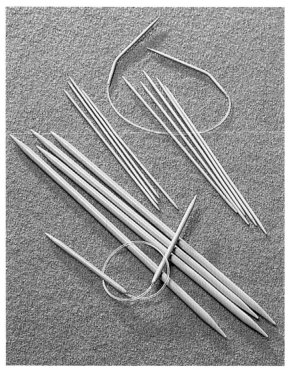

Two-pointed needles

Flexible Single-Pointed Needles

These come in pairs and are made up of a pointed section in the various sizes, followed by a nylon cord of varying lengths, which end in a round disc bearing the size of the needle. These needles allow you to cast on a large number of stitches.

ACCESSORIES

Many accessories are used to make the completion of knitting projects easier. They allow you, among other things, to turn cables, keep stitches in place so you can come back to them when you are doing the finishing touches, prepare yarn for multicolored work, control measurements, or even take notes.

to work back and forth with more stitches than will fit on a straight needle.

Knitting in the round is different from working back and forth. To create stockinette stitch, you just knit round and round. Each full time around is called a round (rnd) rather than a row. To create garter stitch you knit a round, then purl a round. Ribbing is done in the same manner as working back and forth. Working in the round saves you the bother of having to sew the side seams. It is very well suited to two-color knitting, which can be done with one yarn worked with the right hand and the other yarn worked with the left.

Knitting in the round is not recommended for complicated patterns such as Arans, as it is more difficult to take stitches out and replace them on the needle.

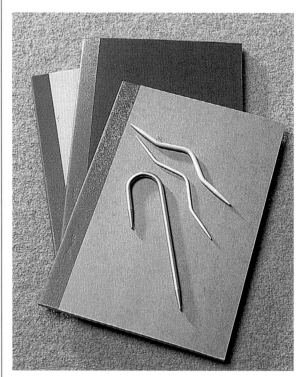

Cable needles

Cable Needles

These are short double-pointed needles with a bend in their middle, or a J-shaped needle with a point at both ends. These serve to hold stitches as you turn a cable.

Needle Gauges and Stitch Holders

Needle gauges allow you to find the size of a needle if the size is not on it. Stitch holders store stitches until they are needed. They are rather like safety pins, without the sharp points, and come in varying lengths to store differing numbers of stitches.

Scissors, Tape Measure, and Pins

Also needed are scissors, a tape measure, pins, and tapestry needles of varying sizes to work yarns

Additional accessories

into the seams. To work smoothly, use a needle with the smallest eye the yarn will pass easily through.

Additional Accessories

You may want point protectors to keep stitches from coming off needles, pegs rather than pins for assembling, row counters, a crochet hook (to pick up a dropped stitch or to cast on the stitches) and bobbins for color knitting.

A notebook is recommended to jot down problems you have met and overcome, the gauge swatch measurements, and a record of the patterns for the piece. This becomes a reference for future works. It is a companion on the journey!

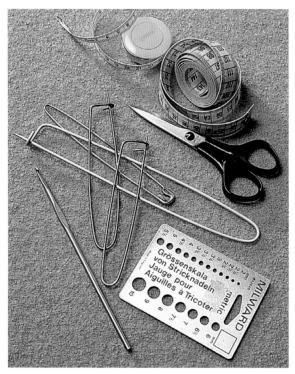

Scissors, needle, gauge, tape measures, and stitch holders

2

Basic Techniques

2. Casting On

TERMINOLOGY

The technical terms used in knitting are very precise, as are their abbreviations, but their usage quickly becomes familiar; the essential maneuvers are repeated endlessly and as a result become nearly automatic. Fully mastering these terms allows you to offer yourself endless pleasure in the creation of original work from the simplest to the most sophisticated.

HOW TO HOLD BASIC SINGLE-POINTED NEEDLES

Generally speaking, short needles are held one in each hand, the right needle held like a pen. With long needles, you can slip the right one under your right arm.

HOW TO HOLD THE YARN BETWEEN YOUR FINGERS

The yarn should be held with an even tension and passed between the fingers to position it on the needle. The regularity, uniformity, and evenness of the knitting depends on this tension. The tension is determined by the yarn's being used and the size of the needles. The information on the skein or ball of yarn and the specifications of the pattern give much help, and it is important, before beginning the work, to make a gauge swatch, to check that you are working to the correct gauge. Change needle sizes if needed to work to the correct gauge.

THE SLIP KNOT

Casting on begins by making a slip knot which will become the first stitch. This slip knot forms the first stitch of all methods of casting on.

I and 2. Hold the end of the yarn tightly in the last three fingers of your left hand, then turn your left hand and pass the yarn over the thumb and index fingers, which should be spaced about 1" (2.5 cm) apart. Hold the yarn from the ball (the working yarn) and the needle in your right hand.

3. Continue to turn your left hand so that the casting on yarn crosses over the working end of the yarn.

4. Insert the point of the needle into this loop, passing under the working end of the yarn, then raise the yarn and bend your index finger to hold it in place.

5. Pass the working end of the yarn around the point of the needle from back to front.

6 and 7. Pass the point of the needle into the loop on the index finger to bring it in front of the work and pull upward to release the stitch.

8. Release the loop from your index finger and pull the thread to tighten the knot formed on the right needle: you have created the slip knot which is the first stitch of the casting on row.

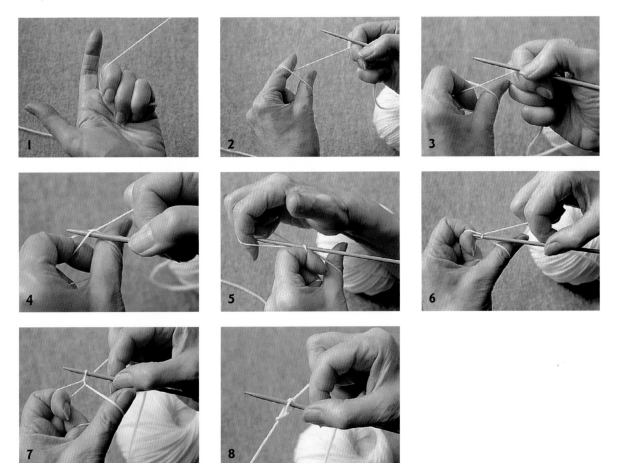

SIMPLE CASTING ON WITH ONE NEEDLE

The casting on row constitutes the foundation of your knitting. It is very important to make this row very carefully because it will help determine the quality of the work, no matter what stitches you will use for the knitted piece.

The simple casting on is made using a single needle, with the first stitch (formed as indicated on the previous page) already placed on the right needle.

1. The yarn coming from the ball of yarn (the working end), serving to cast on the stitches, is held in the left hand, and its hanging end 3" to 4" (7–10 cm) is held in the right hand.

2 and 3. Form a new loop by holding the working end of the yarn between the left thumb and index finger, then turn the left hand to cross the two yarns.

4. Place the point of the right needle in this new loop, passing it under the yarn coming from the needle, and drop it from your index finger.

5. Pull on the working end of the yarn to tighten this new stitch. Form additional stitches in the same manner.

NOTE

The simple casting on, very easy to do, is perfect for openwork stitches and at the beginning of hems because of its near invisibility. It is, however, difficult to obtain a regular and uniform edge.

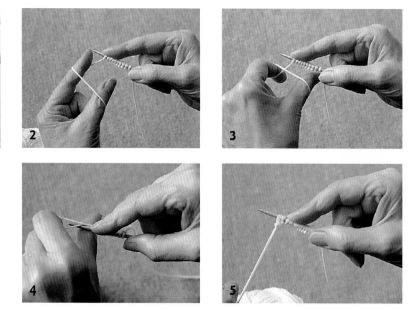

CASTING ON WITH TWO NEEDLES

This method is sometimes called "knitting on." Casting on with two needles begins, just like simple casting on, with a slip knot. This method is most useful when the number of stitches to cast on is quite large. It creates a particularly firm edge.

I. Hold the needle with the first stitch in the left hand, and the second needle with the working end of the yarn in the right hand.

2. Insert the point of the second needle into this first stitch and pass the working end of the yarn from the back to the front, over the needle in your right hand.

3. Then pass the point of the right needle through this stitch to bring the yarn in front and form a new stitch.

4. Slide this new stitch from the right needle to the left needle by placing the point of the left needle around the front of the stitch sliding the new stitch onto the left needle.

5. Remove the right needle, then pull on the working end of the yarn to tighten the newly made stitch. Form the additional stitches in the same manner.

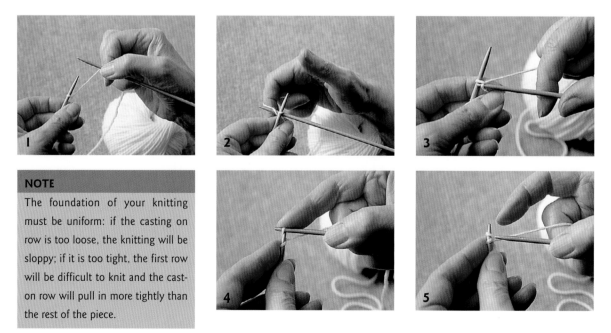

NOTE
The foundation of your knitting must be uniform: if the casting on row is too loose, the knitting will be sloppy; if it is too tight, the first row will be difficult to knit and the cast-on row will pull in more tightly than the rest of the piece.

ITALIAN CASTING ON WITH ONE NEEDLE

Called "Italian casting on," this casting on is done with only one needle, which is held in the right hand. It requires a length of yarn four times the width of the desired knitting project. For example, if the back of the sweater you are knitting is to be 20" (50 cm) in width, the casting on yarn must be 80" (2 m) long.

Once you have carefully measured your length of yarn, hold this in the last three fingers of your left hand and take the working end and the needle in your right hand.

Cast the first stitch onto the right needle as explained earlier.

1 and 2. Hold the yarn between your left thumb and index finger and pivot your left hand to cross the casting on yarn with the working end of the thread.

3. Insert the point of the needle into the loop you have made, passing under the working end of the yarn.

4. Pass the working end of the yarn around the needle, from back to front and then over it.

5–7. Then insert the point of the needle into the loop to bring the yarn to the front of the work. Drop the loop from your index finger and pull the yarn to tighten the new stitch.

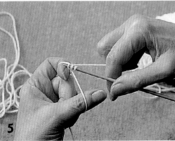

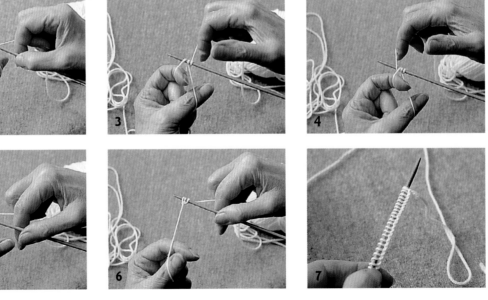

KNIT STITCH

The knit stitch forms a small vertical heart or a "V" on the right side of the work. It is made up of a front loop and a back loop. It is flat and smooth.

1–3. Hold the needle with the stitches in your left hand. Take the second needle in your right hand. Wind the working end of the yarn, held in your right hand, around your right little finger, then pass it under the next two fingers and hold it in place with your index finger.

4. Place the right needle, from front to back, into the first stitch on the left needle.

5 and 6. Pass the working end of the yarn from back to front around the right needle, then pass the point of the needle into the stitch to bring it to the front of the work.

7. Drop the stitch from the left needle. The stitches pass in this manner from the left needle to the right needle along the length of the entire row.

PURL STITCH

The purl stitch is simply the reverse of the knit stitch. Purl stitches form small loops on the surface of the knitting that look like horizontal half-circles. Unlike the knit stitch, it is slightly raised. Purl stitches are generally considered the "wrong" side of the knitted piece.

1. Hold the needle with the stitches in your left hand. Take the second needle in your right hand. Wind the ball of yarn, held in your right hand, around your right little finger, then pass it under the next two fingers and hold it in place with your right index finger. Pass the yarn to the front of the work.

2. Insert the right needle, from back to front, into the first stitch of the left needle.

3. Pass the working end of the yarn around the right needle from top to bottom.

4. Then pass the point of the needle through the stitch to the back of the work.

5. Drop the stitch from the left needle. All stitches pass in this manner from the left needle to the right needle.

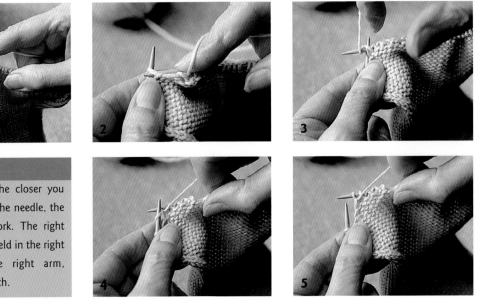

TIP
Generally speaking, the closer you work to the point of the needle, the more quickly you work. The right needle can either be held in the right hand or under the right arm, depending on its length.

The word "selvage" is used to describe each outer edge of a knitted piece, in other words, the first and last stitches of every row. The selvage is most often composed of one stitch, but it can also be worked over two stitches.

Selvages indicate the fine finishing of the knitting. They can have either a decorative or functional look, and if they are even, they make assembling the pieces of a knitting project much easier.

The most often used selvages are the chain selvage, the seam selvage, the single bead selvage, the double bead selvage, and the garter stitch selvage.

THE CHAIN SELVAGE

This selvage forms a chain on the two edges of the knitting; each stitch represents two rows. It is used every time you pick up the stitches on the edge and work in the other direction.

On the knit side, slip the first stitch of the left needle onto the right needle knitwise without knitting it and then knit the last stitch on the row.

On the purl side, slip the first stitch of the needle onto the right needle purlwise without purling it and then purl the last stitch on the purl row.

THE SEAM SELVAGE

This selvage is ideal for beginners because it is the easiest to make. It makes it very easy to sew the side seams together.

Knit the first and the last stitches of the knit row, and then purl the first and last stitches of the purl row.

THE SINGLE BEAD SELVAGE

This selvage is created by always slipping the first stitch knitwise without knitting it and always knitting the second stitch. Do this on each row, on purl rows as well as knit rows.

This selvage is often used for the edges of stockinette stitch because it helps keep the work from curling.

THE DOUBLE BEAD SELVAGE

This selvage is made by knitting the first and last stitch of every row, knit and purl. It is very effective in preventing stockinette stitch from curling. It creates very neat and firm edges.

THE GARTER STITCH SELVAGE

This selvage stitch is used only with garter stitch. It keeps the first stitch of every row from stretching out of shape. Slip the first stitch of every row knitwise with the yarn in front of the row to be worked. Then, you pass the thread to the back of the right needle and knit all the following stitches.

SINGLE INCREASES

Increases allow you to change the size of a knitting project, to enlarge it, to obtain a loose-fitting effect, and to make intricate designs by adding stitches. The most widely-used single increases are the bar increase, the make one increase, the single bead increase, and the yarn over increase.

SINGLE BAR INCREASE

1. On the knit row, plan to increase three stitches from the border at the beginning of the row and at four stitches before the end of the row to create a decorative pattern.

2. Knit the first three stitches without allowing the third to drop from the right needle, then knit this stitch a second time, working it from the back. Drop the stitch from the left needle.

3 and 4. The twisting of the yarn forms a small horizontal base. At the end of the row, when four stitches are left, knit the first of them from the front without dropping the stitch, then knit into the back of the stitch and drop it from the left needle. Knit the remaining three stitches.

TIP

It is better to begin single increases a few stitches in from the edge rather than on the selvage because it keeps the edge from stretching, allows you to find reference points for assembly, and to obtain decorative effects.

SINGLE MAKE ONE INCREASE

1. On the knit row, knit the first three stitches of the row, then with your right needle raise the horizontal bar situated between the third and fourth stitch.

2. Transfer the bar to the left needle, picking it up from front to back. Drop it from the right needle.

3. Knit a stitch in the loop created by raising the bar, and placing the needle in the back of the loop.

4. You have added a stitch whose construction is the same as a single stitch knit in the back.

Repeat the same procedure at the end of the row, before the third stitch from the end, to achieve symmetry.

NOTE

The make one increase is very widely used since it is easily applied to all types of knitting and all types of yarn. It highlights the movement formed for the increase without calling attention to it.

THE SIMPLE BEAD INCREASE

1. On the knit row, knit the first two stitches.

2. Knit the next stitch without dropping it from the left needle.

3 and 4. Pass the yarn to the front of the work, then purl this stitch and drop it from the left needle.

5. Bring the yarn to the back and continue knitting the row.

At the end of the knit row, purl the third stitch before the end, without dropping it from the left needle, and knit it again for symmetry. Knit the final two stitches.

Small holes are formed at each increase.

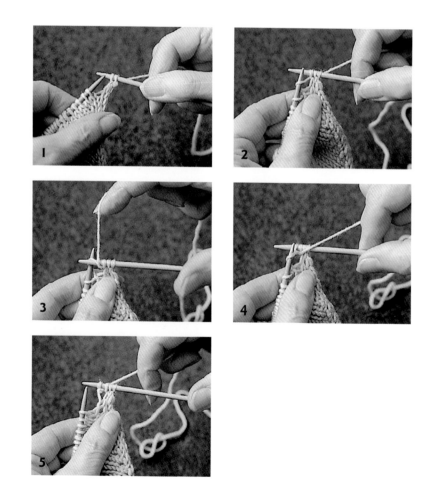

THE SINGLE YARN OVER INCREASE

This increase is made on the knit row with a yarn over which adds an extra stitch. This extra stitch will be worked normally on the next row. This increase leaves a small hole and is used to create a pattern.

1, 2 and 3. Knit the first three stitches of the row. Bring the working yarn under the needle from back to front and back over the needle and continue knitting. Repeat the increase three stitches from the end of the row to create symmetry.

NOTE
The single yarn over stitch increase is often used in layette knitting for baby wear to form a charming added pattern.

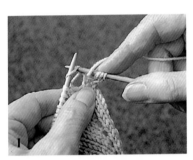

DOUBLE INCREASES

The most common double increases are the double bar increase, the double make one increase, and the double yarn over increase. They are made like single increases, but in specific places. The double increase is separated by a center stitch which is the center of these increases.

THE DOUBLE BAR INCREASE

1 and 2. On the knit row, the first increase is made as a single bar increase. Make a knit stitch before the center stitch without dropping it from the needle.

3. Then knit into the back of the stitch.

4. Drop the stitch from the left needle.

5. Repeat this procedure for the center stitch.

6. A small bar has been formed on each side of the center stitch.

Purl the following row normally. The following increases are always made in the stitch which precedes the center stitch and in the center stitch itself.

THE DOUBLE MAKE ONE INCREASE

1 and 2. On the knit row, with your right needle, catch the bar which precedes the center stitch; transfer the bar onto the left needle.

3 and 4. Knit a stitch by placing the needle into the back of the loop formed by this action, then knit the center stitch normally.

5. Repeat this step by catching the bar found after the center stitch, place the loop on the left needle and knit a stitch in the back of this new stitch.

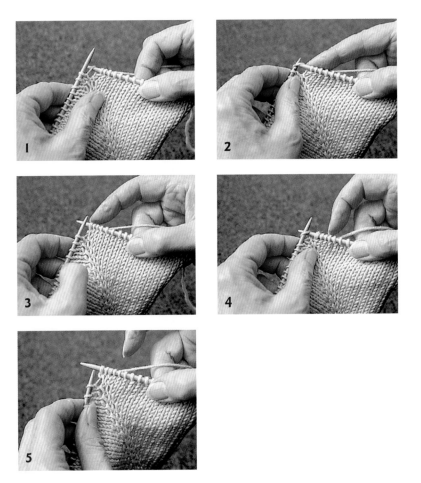

THE DOUBLE YARN OVER INCREASE

1–3. On the knit row, yarn over before knitting the center stitch; knit this stitch, then yarn over again and continue knitting until the end of the row.

On the purl row, purl all the stitches including the yarn over stitches.

NOTE

Yarn over increases often form one of the bases for openwork or lace stitches. They are accompanied by parallel double decreases which allows you to re-establish the balance of the number of stitches by bringing you back to the number of stitches cast on at the beginning.

2. Decreases

SIMPLE DECREASES

Decreases allow you to reduce the size of a knitting project, to modify it in desired places by eliminating stitches. Decreases combined with yarn over increases form the basis of lace knitting stitches. They are usually made on the knit row, at the beginning and end of the row, and the next row is then purled as normal: we speak of decreases being made every other row. To obtain symmetrical effects on the same row, they slant either to the right or to the left.

KNIT DECREASE, SLANTING TO THE LEFT

1. On the front of the work, on the edge or a few stitches from the edge (for a decorative or structured look), slip a stitch onto the right needle. Knit the next stitch.

2 and 3. Using the left needle, lift and bring the slipped stitch over the knitted stitch. Drop the passed slip stitch from the needle.

4. This decrease slants to the left. It is a single slipped stitch. The next row is then purled as normal.

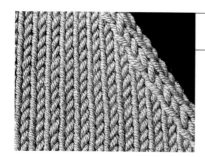

KNIT DECREASE, SLANTING TO THE RIGHT

1. On the front of the work, knit the stitches until the end of the row, or stop a few stitches from the end (duplicating on the decrease at the beginning of the row).

2 and 3. Work two stitches together by inserting the right needle first into the second stitch and then into the first, and knit them together.

4. This decrease slants to the right. It assures a symmetry with the single slipped stitch. The next row is purled as normal.

IMPORTANT

For a finished look to the knitting, it is important to use the left and right slanting decreases as appropriate at the beginning and end of the row.

PURL DECREASE, SLANTING TO THE RIGHT

1 and 2. On the back of the work, the decrease which will be slanting to the right on the front of the work is made by working two stitches together purlwise, inserting the right needle into the first and then into the second stitch.

PURL DECREASE, SLANTING TO THE LEFT

1–3. This decrease will be slanted to the left on the right side of the work. With the left needle, take the last stitch worked from the right needle; pass the next stitch on the left needle over this stitch, drop it, and place the remaining stitch back on the right needle. The following row is knitted normally.

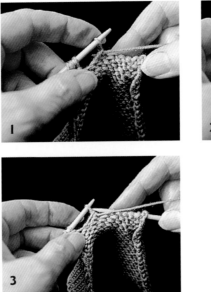

DOUBLE DECREASES

A double decrease reduces by two stitches at one time. It is done, for example, to form the point of a collar. Combined with yarn overs, it can be used to create decorative effects.

DOUBLE KNIT DECREASE, LEFT SLANT

I and 2. Knit three stitches together knitwise, taking them in order and inserting the right needle into the first, then into the second and finally into the third.

3. Drop the decrease from the left needle. The following row is purled as normal.

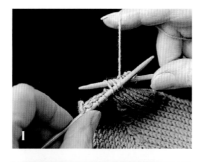

DOUBLE KNIT DECREASE, RIGHT SLANT

1 and 2. Knit three stitches together knitwise, taking them from the front and inserting the needle in the third, then the second and finally in the first stitch.

Drop the decrease from the left needle. The following row is purled as normal.

DOUBLE KNIT DECREASE OVERLAPPING TO THE LEFT

1. Slip a stitch knitwise, then insert the needle into the next two stitches, beginning with the second stitch.

2. Knit these two stitches together knitwise.

3. Bring the slipped stitch over the decrease stitch you just made and drop it. The following row is purled as normal.

DOUBLE KNIT DECREASE OVERLAPPING TO THE RIGHT

1. Slip a stitch knitwise onto the right needle.

2. Knit a knitwise stitch and bring the slipped stitch over this stitch.

3. Slip it back onto the left needle, then slip the next stitch from the left needle over this stitch.

4. Bring the stitch back to the right needle. The following row is purled as normal.

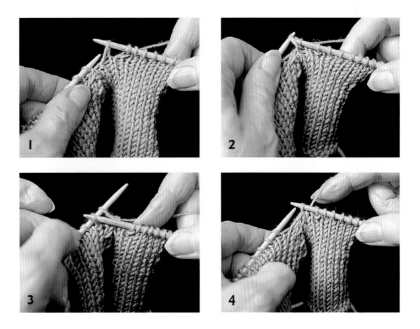

DOUBLE KNIT VERTICAL DECREASE

1 and 2. Slip two stitches together knitwise onto the right needle, inserting first into the second stitch and then into the first.

3 and 4. Knit the following stitch knitwise, then bring the two slipped stitches over the knitted stitch, dropping them.

YARN OVER STITCHES

A yarn over stitch adds one or more stitches on a single row. It does not add stitches when it is followed by a similar amount of decreased stitches.

A yarn over stitch plays a decorative role: it forms an openwork design.

YARN OVER BETWEEN KNITTED STITCHES

The yarn is at the back of the knitting.

1 and 2. Bring the yarn to the front of the work, then pass over the needle from front to back.

3. Knit the next stitch as usual.

4–6. On the purl row, purl the yarn over by inserting the needle in the loop of the stitch. A stitch has been added forming a little hole.

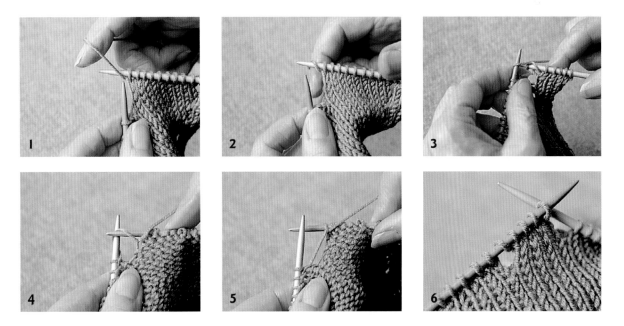

YARN OVER BETWEEN PURL STITCHES

I and 2. Bring the yarn to the front of the work, then wrap it around the needle and bring it back to the front.

3. Purl the following stitch as normal; a stitch is added forming a little hole.

SLIPPED STITCHES

SINGLE SLIPPED STITCH

The simple decrease slanted to the left is also called the single slipped stitch.

- Slip a stitch knitwise from the left needle to the right needle.
- Knit the following stitch, then bring the slipped stitch over the knit stitch.

DOUBLE SLIPPED STITCH

- Slip a stitch knitwise from the left needle to the right needle.
- Knit the next two stitches together, then bring the slipped stitch over the stitch resulting from the knit two together.

Binding off, sometimes called casting off, completes the work by keeping the stitches from coming undone after they have left the needle. The stitches on the last row are bound one by one in different ways according to the part of the knitting to be bound off (shoulder, neck, button hole). It is important to bind off with care so that you obtain a smooth and uniform border.

On the knit side, the stitches are usually bound off knitwise. On the purl side, they are bound off purlwise. For ribbing or other patterns, the stitches are bound off following the existing pattern.

REGULAR BINDING OFF

This binding off is the most common and easiest to do. The stitches leapfrog over each other knitwise on the front and purlwise on the back.

I. Knit the first two stitches.

2 and 3. With the point of the left needle, lift the first stitch over the second and drop it. There is only one stitch remaining on the right needle. Knit a new stitch and lift the first over the second, continue until there is only the final stitch on the right needle.

Cut the thread, leaving a long enough strand to be able to work it back into the knitting. Pass the cut end through the last stitch and pull tightly: the final stitch is thus secured.

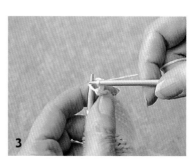

ENGLISH BINDING OFF

The stitches of this binding off interlock knitwise on the knit side and purlwise on the purl.

1 and 2. Knit two stitches together, inserting the needle into the back loops.

3. Replace the resulting stitch onto the left needle, then knit it together with the next stitch, as you did for the first two, inserting the needle onto the back loops.

This method allows you to obtain a firm, sturdy finish by closing up the knitting. It works particularly well for shoulder seams, pocket edges, and for finishing cable stitches.

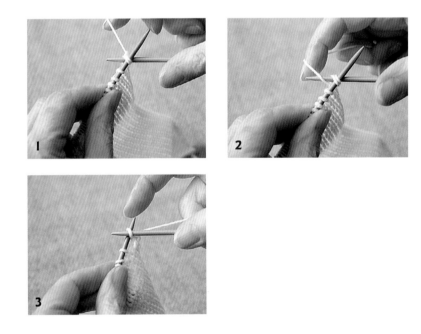

VARIATION

To maintain the elasticity of a patterned edge, bind off the stitches of the final row in the regular manner by working them as they are presented. In other words, knitting the knit stitches and purling the purl stitches, lifting one ever the other. This binding off, allows you to finish the stitches more flexibly than if all were worked in knit or purl.

FANCY BINDING OFF

BELGIAN BINDING OFF ON STOCKINETTE

To create a decorative effect on the front of the piece, work the stitches on the last purl row of the work by knitting them.

1. Knit the first two stitches; bring the first stitch over the second.
2 and 3. Continue in this manner until all the stitches are worked. Finish the last stitch as for regular bind off.

BELGIAN BINDING OFF ON GARTER STITCH

The principle of this binding off is to work all the stitches knitwise on the back of the work.

1. Knit the first two stitches.
2. Bring the first stitch over the second.
3. Continue in this manner until all stitches are bound off.

  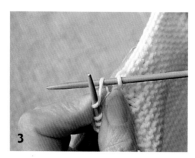

THE FINAL KNOT

The slip knot forms the first stitch beginning the casting on, and the final knot marks the end of each piece made.

I and 2. To secure the last stitch remaining on the needle, enlarge the loop in order to pass the working end of the yarn through it.
3. Then pull it through the loop to form the final knot. Trim the working end of the yarn to about 6 inches (15 cm).

TIP

You can also bind off the stitches with a crochet hook and chaining through the stitches. You choose the size of the crochet hook to match the size of the needles used, or use a larger size if you wish to obtain a looser final row.

KNITTING IN THE ROUND USING A SET OF 4 OR 5 DOUBLE-POINTED NEEDLES

Knitting in the round allows you to eliminate side and sleeve seams. The set of four 7-inch, double-pointed needles is generally used for socks, mittens, gloves, or hats. For a piece with more stitches, it is easier to use a set of five needles. Sets of four and five needles come in both 7- and 10-inch lengths.

1 and 2. Leave one needle of the set empty for a working needle. Cast on the stitches, distributed evenly on the remaining needles.

3. On three needles, they naturally form a triangle. On four needles, they form a square. Be sure stitches are not twisted on needle.

4. With the empty needle, knit across the first needle. Each newly emptied needle becomes the working needle to knit across the next needle as you work around. Join the last stitch to the first stitch.

5. Continue to work around on each needle, using the previous needle as the working needle and guiding the working yarn with your right hand.

To work a gauge swatch, work back and forth on two needles.

NOTE
Knitting in the round or circular knitting is defined in terms of "rounds" rather than "rows."

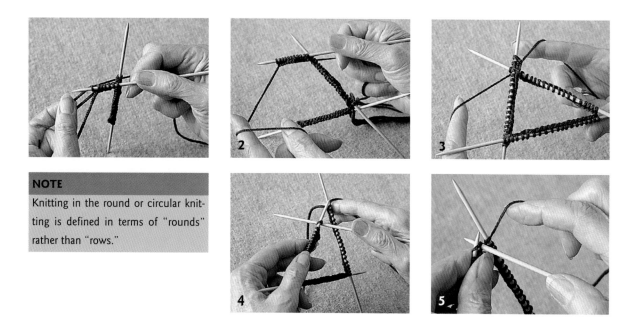

KNITTING IN THE ROUND USING A CIRCULAR NEEDLE

This method of working has come to us much more recently, with Anglo-Saxon and Germanic knitting methods. Before anything else, make sure that the length of the needle (which is printed on the package) corresponds to the knitting to be done. A hat is done with a 16 inch needle, a sweater with a 24 or 29 inch one. The stitches must fit without stress on the needle in order to slide easily. If the needle is too long, the stitches will be pulled out of shape and be distorted. A shorter needle, on the other hand, will make the work easier, with the stitches gliding naturally. Mark the beginning of each round so you know where the next round begins.

1. Cast on the number of stitches needed to make the pattern, and mark the first stitch. The tail from casting on, if you have used a two needle method, can serve as this marker. Be sure the stitches are not twisted around the needle.

2. Join the first stitch to the last with the working end of the yarn, then continue: a circle of stitches is formed on the needle.

In this manner, knit the rounds one after the other. The work is very easy if the length of the needle is appropriate to the number of stitches.

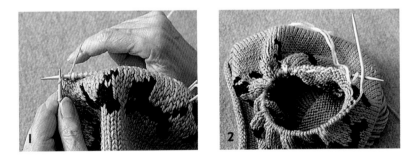

Errors or blunders in knitting are easy to correct. If a stitch drops from the needle and it runs, forming a little ladder, you can "fish it out" and bring it back to its position on the row from which it escaped.

PICKING UP A DROPPED STITCH ON THE RIGHT SIDE WITH A CROCHET HOOK

1–3. On the right side of the piece, place the crochet hook in the stitch that has dropped, then pass it under the bar situated directly above and pull the yarn through the stitch. Repeat this as many times as needed to "climb" all the rungs of the ladder to the row in progress.

If the purl side is the right side, turn the piece before working and pick the stitch up from the knit side.

PICKING UP A DROPPED STITCH ON THE KNIT SIDE WITH A NEEDLE

If you observe that a stitch has been poorly knitted on a previous row, that it is twisted or in error (a knit on the purl row or a purl on the knit row, for example), you must first unravel the stitch column down to the place where you made the mistake. Then insert the right needle in this stitch and pass it under the horizontal bar situated directly above, then insert the left needle into the stitch and bring it over the bar; it is always worked on the right needle.

For the following rows, simply pass the needle under the bar and bring the stitch over it. When the work is finished, slide the stitch on the left needle and knit it.

PICKING UP A DROPPED PURL STITCH

Generally, it is easier to turn the work and pick up the stitch from the knit side, but if it is necessary to work on the purl side:

1. Insert the right needle into the stitch, from the back to the front, also passing it under the bar situated directly above.

2 and 3. Insert the left needle in the stitch from front to back, passing behind the yarn, and bring the stitch over the bar.

Repeat this procedure as many times as needed to bring the stitch back to the last worked row. If you have many stitches to repair, it is easier to undo the knitting completely to the point where the error was made and then re-knit the unraveled part.

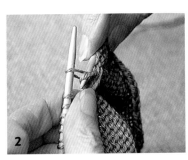

ADDING A NEW BALL OF YARN

Adding a new ball of yarn is done every time you come to the end of the yarn you are using.

1. Attaching the new ball of yarn is usually done at the beginning of a row.

2 and 3. Leaving at least a 6-inch (15 centimeter) end on each ball, knit the first stitch with both yarns, then continue with only the new yarn. Knot the two yarns together in a square knot since this is the flattest knot; then, when the piece is finished, weave the ends into the knitting with a tapestry needle.

If you must join a new ball in the middle of a row, work as above, but do not tie the knot for three or four rows so that you can adjust the tension and make sure the stitches are all of proper size.

 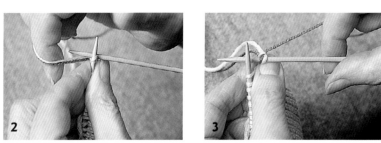

CHOOSING THE SIZE

How do you choose your size from the sizes given in the directions? Usually, the directions in patterns are available in a number of sizes; the number of stitches is usually indicated for the smallest size, and in parentheses for larger sizes. Choose the size that best fits your measurements.

2. The Gauge Swatch

The gauge swatch is a vital element and determinant for your knitting. It allows you to adjust the number of stitches and rows, to define in the best way the relationship between the size of the needles, the chosen yarn and the tension of the knitter. The way of holding the yarn, the tension of the stitches, etc., varies from knitter to knitter. Consequently, it is important to make a gauge swatch in order to see the surface and then to compare the size with the number of stitches and rows using the size needles called for. This information will be both on the paper around the yarn (the yarn band) and at the beginning of the pattern under the heading "Gauge."

If the number of stitches (or rows) of your gauge swatch is smaller than the dimensions given in the directions for the size (in general, 4 inches [or 10 cm]), you must use larger needles. If, on the other hand, it is larger, you just use smaller needles. It is easier to change the size of the needles than to change, by hand, the tension of the thread and the tightness of the stitches.

1. Lightly steam the gauge swatch to obtain a square that is 4 inches (10 centimeters) on each side. Stitches and rows are measured using a tape measure and a large pin.

2. First count the stitches one by one across the same row, marking with a colored thread the two ends of the 4-inch (10 cm) gauge swatch.

3. Count the rows on the same vertical column and mark with a colored thread the two extremities of the 4-inch (10 cm) gauge swatch.

Always make a new gauge swatch for each knitting project and for each series of different stitches.

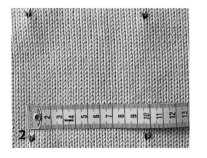
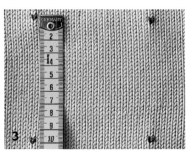

3

Knitting Stitches

The Basic Stitches

The variety of ways of combining knit and purl stitches is so vast that it is nearly impossible to describe them all. Our choice is based and classified on categories of stitches in small groups which gives you access to a very wide range of possibilities. The basic stitches are the most frequently used and the easiest to make, and all other existing stitches stem from these, from the most simple to the most complex. They are always made up of knitted and purled stitches. You knit the first row, turn the work, and then either knit or purl, as directed the second row, always trying to keep the tension of the yarn even. The easiest basic stitches are the garter stitch and the stockinette and reverse stockinette stitch.

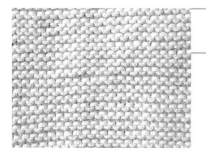

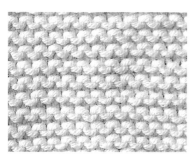

THE GARTER STITCH

The garter stitch is the stitch that beginners learn before any other: it is the easiest to do. It has a raised appearance that is identical on the front and the back.

It is knitted over a span of any number of stitches.

Row 1: Knit.

Row 2: Knit.

Repeat these two rows. The two rows form what is called a "ridge." When counting, one ridge is two rows.

NOTE

You should always finish the row you are working on before stopping the knitting: this will prevent errors and a change in tension in the middle of the row.

THE STOCKINETTE STITCH

This stitch alternates rows of knit stitches and purl stitches.

The front of the work features a smooth and uniform surface where the stitches form a small heart or "V." On the back of the work, the surface features loops which form horizontal half circles. Considering the smooth and uniform surface on both sides, we have the "stockinette stitch" (photos 1 and 2), and, if we turn the work over, we have the "reverse stockinette stitch" (photos 3 and 4).

The stockinette stitch can be combined over any number of stitches.

Row 1: Knit.

Row 2: Purl.

Repeat these two rows.

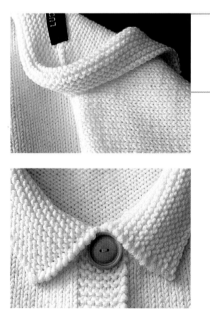

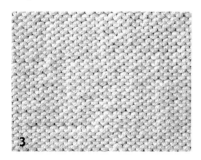

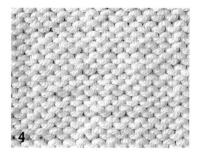

VARIATIONS ON GARTER AND STOCKINETTE STITCHES

The garter stitch perfectly alternates with the stockinette stitch, as we see in this example where it decorates the neck and the borders of a small baby's cardigan knitted in the stockinette stitch.

Baby Blanket and Bootees

BOOTEES

Size:
3–6 months

Materials:
1.75 ounces (50 grams) of sport weight yarn in the color of your choice.
Pair size 3 (3-1/4 mm) needles

Stitch used:
Garter stitch: K every row.

Gauge Swatch:
24 stitches and 48 rows = 4" (10 cm) in garter stitch using size 3 needles

BLANKET

Size:
23-1/2" x 31-1/2" (60 x 80 cm)

Materials:
9 ounces (250 grams) sport weight wool in the color of your choice
Pair size 4 (3.5 mm) needles

Stitches used:
Garter stitch: all rows are knitted
Stockinette stitch:
K one row, P one row

Gauge:
22 stitches and 30 rows = 4" (10 cm)

INSTRUCTIONS

BOOTEES

Begin with the sole: Cast on 16 stitches. K 1 row, working in garter stitch and working 2 stitches in from edge, increase 1 stitch at the beginning and end of row. Work 3 rows even, increase as before on 1 row, work 3 rows even, increase on 1 row, 22 stitches. K 10 rows even. Again working 2 stitches from edges, decrease 1 stitch at each end of every fourth row 3 times, 16 stitches.

Continue on upper part of bootees: Cast on 8 more stitches for half of the heel extension. Work in garter stitch across all stitches and working 2 stitches in from toe end, increase 1 stitch every fourth row 3 times, 27 stitches. End at heel. Bind off 14 stitches. K 10 rows even on remaining 13 stitches. Cast on 14 stitches for other half of heel extension. Work in garter stitch and, working 2 stitches from toe edge, decrease 1 stitch every fourth row 3 times to correspond to previous toe increases. Bind off the remaining 24 stitches.

FINISHING TOUCHES

Sew adjoining edges of heel extensions together, forming a loop. Sew bound-off stitches, toe and heel sections to the sole.

TIP

Make two pompons (see page 184) and sew them on the instep or at the back of the bootie for a finishing touch. Be sure they are firmly attached.

BLANKET

With number 4 (3.5 mm) needles, cast on 132 stitches. K 1" (3 cm) in garter stitch. Next row: K #1, P to last #1 stitches, K #1. Row 2: K. Repeat last two rows until piece measures 22-1/2" (76.5 cm). Work in garter stitch for 1" (3 cm). Bind off. Block lightly.

Fuzzy Cap and Bootees with Pompons

BONNET AND SHOES

Size:
3–6 months

Materials:
1-3/4 oz. (50 g) of sport weight yarn in off-white and pale yellow or as desired, 2 small buttons
Pair size 3 (3-1/4 mm) needles, tapestry needle

Stitch used:
Garter stitch: K every row.

Gauge Swatch:
24 sts and 44 rows = 4" (10 cm) in garter st using size 3 needles

INSTRUCTIONS

CAP

Cast on 82 sts and K 5" (13 cm) in garter stitch, then shape top of cap by dec 10 sts across the row as follows: *K 6 sts, K 2 tog*, rep between the * and * 10 times, (72 sts).

Repeat these dec every 4th row 6 times, having 1 less st between dec each row.

Cut yarn leaving an end long enough to sew seam. Thread tapestry needle with yarn end and draw remaining 12 sts together; pull tight and fasten. Sew seam. Turn up bottom edge for cuff.

Make a small pompon (see page 184) and sew to the top of the bonnet.

BOOTEES

Work same as bootees on page 60. After sewing together, make straps as follows:

For the strap, cast on 22 sts, then pick up and knit the 16 sts from the heel extension, then cast on another 6 stitches, 44 sts. K 6 rows in garter st making a buttonhole on the third row: K 2, K 2 tog, yarn over, work rem sts. Work the next 3 rows even. Bind off.

Work the second strap in the same manner, working the buttonhole at the end of the row rather than the beg. Sew a button opposite each buttonhole. Make 2 small pompons and sew 1 to the front of each bootee.

TIP

To make a larger cap, cast on 8 additional stitches and make 11 decreases. To make a smaller cap, cast on 8 stitches fewer and make 9 decreases.

Child's Sweater in Garter and Stockinette Stitches

SWEATER

Size:
4 years

Materials:
11 ozs (300 g) sport weight yarn in the color of your choice
Pair each sizes 3 (3-1/4 mm) and 4 (3.5 mm) needles

Stitches used:
Garter stitch: K every row
Stockinette stitch: K one row, P one row.

Gauge swatch:
With large needles 22sts and 32 rows = 4" (10 cm) in St st

INSTRUCTIONS

BACK

With large needles, cast on 96 sts and work in garter st for 1" (3 cm), continue in St st.

Work even until pieces measures 6-3/4" (17 cm), place markers at either side. Continue to work even until piece measures 18" (45 cm) from beg. Bind off 30 sts at each side and place center 36 sts on a stitch holder for neck.

FRONT

Work same as back until piece measures 15-1/2" (39 cm).

Work 43 sts, place next 10 st on a holder for neck shaping, attach a second ball of yarn and working both sides at the same time, bind off 3 sts at the neck edge at the beg of the next 4 rows, 2 sts at the beg of the next 4 rows. Then, with RS facing, dec at each neck edge as follows: K to the last 4 sts of the first side, K 2 tog, K 2; on the second side, K 2, SKP, K to end of row. Next row, P. Rep these 2 rows 2 times more (30 sts). When front measures same as back, bind off.

SLEEVES

With larger needles, cast on 54 sts and work in garter st for 1" (3 cm). Continue in St st increasing every 6th row 11 times as follows: K 2, inc, work to the last 3 sts, inc, work last 2 sts. (76 sts). When piece measure 9-1/2" (24 cm), bind off all sts.

FINISHING TOUCHES

Lightly block the pieces.

Sew the left shoulder. K the 36 stitches from the back of the neck onto one of the smaller needles, pick up and K 17 sts along the left front of the neck edge. K the 10 sts from the neck front, pick up and K 17 stitches on the second side. Work 5 rows st st (these rows will curl over, creating a rev ST st collar); bind off. Sew the second shoulder and the edge of the collar. Sew sleeves between markers then sew sleeve and side seams with a stitch to stitch seam (see page 193).

Tunic

THE TUNIC

Size:
Medium

Materials:
25 ozs (700 g) worsted weight
yarn in the color of your choice
One pair each size 6 (4-1/4 mm)
and 8 (5 mm) needles

Stitches used:
1x1 rib st: K 1, P 1.
Stockinette stitch (St st): Knit one
row, purl one row.

Gauge swatch:
With large needles 16 sts and 22
rows = 4" (10 cm) in St st.

INSTRUCTIONS

BACK

With smaller needles cast on 91 sts. Work 2" (5 cm) in 1x1 rib. Change to larger needles and work in St st until piece measures 27-1/2" (70 cm) from beg.

Work the shoulders and the neck at the same time as follows: For each shoulder, bind off 8 stitches every other row 3 times and place the center 33 stitches on a holder for neck. Work each side separately. At each neck edge dec 1 st each row 5 times.

FRONT

Work as for back until piece measures 25" (65 cm). Place the center 19 sts on a holder then working each side separately on 36 sts at neck edge, bind off 3 sts once, 2 sts twice, then dec 1 st every row three times.

When front measures same length as back, bind off same as back. Work second side.

At 27-1/2" (70 cm) in total length, bind off the shoulders in the same way as you did the ones on the back (8 stitches every other row 3 times).

SLEEVES

With smaller needles, cast on 51 sts, work in 1x1 rib for 2" (5 cm). Change to larger needles. Working in St st, inc 1 st at each side, 2 sts from edge, every other row 5 times, then every 6th row 8 times, (77 sts).

Work even until piece measures 15-1/2" (39 cm) ending with a wrong side row. Bind off 10 sts at the beg of the next 2 rows. Bind off 7 sts at the beg of the next 6 rows.

FINISHING TOUCHES

Sew the left shoulder. With smaller needles, pick up the 5 sts on the back neck edge, then pick up the 33 sts from the back holder, pick up the 5 sts on the second side, then 18 sts along the edge of the front neck edge. Then pick up the 19 sts from the center front holder and pick up 18 sts along the second side, (98 sts).

Knit 1" (3 cm) in 1x1 rib. Bind off the stitches as worked. Sew the second shoulder and the edge of the neck.

Open piece flat. Place markers 9-1/2" (24 cm) down from the shoulder seams. Center sleeves between markers and sew in place. Sew side and sleeve seams. Block lightly.

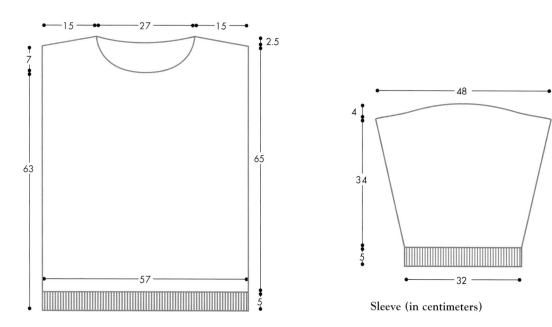

Front and Back (in centimeters)

Sleeve (in centimeters)

Mohair Sweater with Cat's Tooth Stitch Sleeves

THE SWEATER

Size:
Medium

Materials:
6 ozs (150 g) sport weight mohair in the color of your choice
Pairs needles size 1 (2-3/4 mm), 3 (3-1/4 mm), and 6 (4-1/4 mm)

Stitches used:
Stockinette stitch: K 1 row, P 1 row.
Cat's tooth stitch: Row 1: Selvage stitch. *K 2 tog, yo*; repeat * to *; end 1 selvage stitch. Row 2: P across.

Gauge swatch:
With medium needles 24 sts and 34 rows = 4" (10 cm)

CREATE IT

BACK

With medium needles, cast on 120 sts and work in St st for 1" (13 cm) for the hem, then work 1 row of rev St st and then work another 1" (13 cm) of St st.

To fold the hem, pick up the 120 cast-on sts with a medium needle and knit one row with largest needles, taking one stitch from each needle and working them together.

With largest needles continue in St st and dec 1 st at each edge, working 2 sts in from edge, every fourth row 11 times; on right, knit 2 sts tog; on left, skp. Then inc 1 st at each edge, again 2 sts from edges, 11 times, alternating every 4 and 6 rows (2 inc on 10 rows).

At 14" (36 cm) from the beg, bind off 5 sts at the beg of the next 2 rows, 3 sts at the beg of the next 2 rows, 2 sts at the beg of the next 6 rows, then dec 1 st each side every other row 3 times, (86 sts).

When the piece measures 22" (56 cm) from the turned up hem, begin the shoulder and neck shaping. Bind off 8 sts at the beg of the next 6 rows. Place the center 28 sts on a holder. Working each side separately, bind off the rem 5 sts at each neck edge.

FRONT

Work as for back.

At 18" (46 cm) from the turned up hem, place the center 18 sts on a holder for the neck. Finish each side separately, binding off 3 sts at each neck edge once, then 2 sts every other row 2 times, then dec 1 st every other row 3 times.

When front measures same as back, work shoulder shaping.

SLEEVES

NOTE

The sleeves here are three-quarter length.

With medium needles, cast on 60 sts. Work 4 rows in St st. Work 2 rows of cat's tooth stitch (see box at left). Work 4 more rows of St st.

Change to largest needles. Continue in St st and inc 1 st each side every 6th row 13 times, (86 sts). When piece measures 10-1/2" (27 cm) from beg, shape cap as follows: Bind off 3 sts at beg of next 2 rows, then 3 sts at beg of next 2 rows. Dec 1 st at beg and end of every 4th row 6 times. Then bind off 2 sts at beg of every 3rd and 4th row 4 times, bind off 2 sts at beg of next 6 rows, 3 sts at beg of next 2 rows, 4 sts at beg of next 2 rows. Bind off rem 18 sts.

FINISHING TOUCHES

Block lightly if desired.

Sew the left shoulder. With smallest needles, pick up and K 5 sts on right back neckline, then 28 center sts from holder, 5 sts on left back, 11 sts on left front to holder, 18 sts from front holder, 11 on right front to shoulder.

Work 5 rows in St st. Bind off all sts. Seam the right shoulder and neckband edge.

Sew the sides. Seam the sleeves and attach them to the sweater.

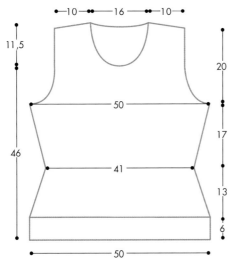

Back and Front (in centimeters)

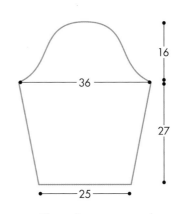

Sleeve (in centimeters)

Variations on Basic Stitches

The following variations on basic stitches make them more imaginative; they are composed of knit stitches and purl stitches combined in a variety of different ways. These stitches are categorized according to their appearance or their structure.

The stitches are a set of stitches treated as a single unit, repeated until the end of the row and contained within asterisks (*) to make the instructions easier to read. We also list the number of rows required to form the pattern.

THE SEED STITCH

The seed stitch, also known as the moss stitch, is made by alternately working a knit stitch and a purl stitch on the same row, then doing the opposite on the next row.

Row 1: * Knit 1, purl 1 *; repeat from * to *.
Row 2: Alternate the stitches by working a purl stitch directly above a knit one and a knit stitch directly above a purl one. Repeat these two rows.

VARIATION ON THE SEED STITCH

For this stitch, diamonds and panels of seed stitch are alternated, separated by rib panels. This motif is worked over 41 stitches plus 1 selvage stitch at the beginning and end of each row.

Row 1: 1 selvage st, P 2 sts, K 2 sts, work 7 sts in seed st, K 2 sts, P 2 sts, K 11 sts, P 2 sts, K 2 sts, work 7 sts in seed st, K 2 sts, P 2 sts, 1 selvage st.

Row 2: 1 selvage st, K 2 sts, P 2 sts, work 7 sts in seed st, P 2 sts, K 2 sts, P 11 sts, K 2 sts, P 2 sts, work 7 sts in seed st, P 2 sts, K 2 sts, 1 selvage st.

Row 3: 1 selvage st, P 2 sts, K 2 sts, work 7 sts in seed st, K 2 sts, P 2 sts, K 11 sts, P 2 sts, K 2 sts, work 7 sts in seed st, K 2 sts, P 2 sts, 1 selvage st.

Row 4: 1 selvage st, K 2 sts, P 2 sts, work 7 sts in seed st, P 2 sts, K 2 sts, P 5 sts, K 1 st (this forms the base of the diamond), P 5 sts, K 2 sts, P 2 sts, work 7 sts in seed st, P 2 sts, K 2 sts, 1 selvage stitch.

Row 5: 1 selvage st, P 2 sts, K 2 sts, 7 sts in seed st, K 2 sts, P 2 sts, K 4 sts, 3 sts in seed st (P 1 st, K 1 st, P 1 st), K 4 sts, P 2 sts, K 2 sts, 7 sts in seed st, K 2 sts, P 2 sts, 1 selvage stitch.

Row 6: 1 selvage st, K 2 sts, P 2 sts, work 7 sts in seed st, P 2 sts, K 2 sts, P 3 sts, work 5 sts in seed st, P 3 sts, K 2 sts, P 2 sts, work 7 sts in seed st, P 2 sts, K 2 sts, 1 selvage st.

Row 7: 1 selvage st, P 2 sts, K 2 sts, work 7 sts in seed st, K 2 sts, P 2 sts, K 2 sts, work 7 sts in seed st, K 2 sts, P 2 sts, K 2 sts, work 7 sts in seed st, K 2 sts, P 2 sts, 1 selvage st.

Row 8: 1 selvage st, K 2 sts, P 2 sts, work 7 sts in seed st, P 2 sts, K 2 sts, P 1 st, work 9 sts in seed st, P 2 st, K 2 sts, P 2 sts, work 7 sts in seed st, P 2 sts, K 2 sts, 1 selvage st.

Row 9: 1 selvage st, P 2 sts, K 2 sts, work 7 sts in seed st, K 2 sts, P 2 sts, K 2 sts, work 7 sts in seed st, K 2 sts, P 2 sts, K 2 sts, work 7 sts in seed st, K 2 sts, P 2 sts, 1 selvage st.

Row 10: 1 selvage st, K 2 sts, P 2 sts, work 7 sts in seed st, P 2 sts, K 2 sts, P 3 sts, work 5 sts in seed st, P 3 sts, K 2 sts, P 2 sts, work 7 sts in seed st, P 2 sts, K 2 sts, 1 selvage st.

Row 11: 1 selvage st, P 2 sts, K 2 sts, work 7 sts in seed st, K 2 sts, P 2 sts, K 4 sts, work 3 sts in seed st, K 4 sts, P 2 sts, K 2 sts, work 7 sts in seed st, K 2 sts, P 2 sts, 1 selvage st.

Row 12: 1 selvage st, K 2 sts, P 2 sts, work 7 sts in seed st, P 2 sts, K 2 sts, P 5 sts, K 1 st (seed st), P 5 sts, K 2 sts, P 2 sts, work 7 sts in seed st, P 2 sts, K 2 sts, 1 selvage st.

Repeat these twelve rows.

DOUBLE MOSS STITCH

The number of stitches must be in multiples of 2.

Row 1: : * K 1 st, P 1 st *.
Row 2: K the ks and P the ps.
Row 3: * Purl 1 st, Knit 1 st *.
Row 4: P the ps and K the ks.
Repeat these four rows.

THE CHECKERBOARD STITCH

This stitch is made up of many knit and purl stitches knitted in opposition after a certain number of rows. The number of stitches must be in multiple of 4, plus 1 selvage stitch at the beginning and end of the row.

Row 1: 1 selvage st, *K 2 sts, P 2 sts*, repeat from * to *; end 1 selvage st.
Row 2 and all the even rows: Work the stitches as the row before.
Row 3: Work the stitches as in row 1.
Row 5: 1 selvage st, *P 2 sts, K 2 sts*, repeat from * to *; end 1 selvage st.
Row 7: Work the stitches as indicated in row 5.
Repeat these eight rows.

NOTE
You can create larger checkerboard squares, 4/4 or 6/6, for example.

THE WELT STITCH

This stitch creates a deep texture at regular intervals on the stockinette stitch. To obtain this depth, you work one or more rows of reverse stockinette on the right side. The number of stitches does not matter.

Version for 6 rows:

Row 1: Knit.

Row 2: Purl.

Row 3: Knit.

Row 4: Knit.

Row 5: Purl.

Row 6: Knit.

Repeat these six rows.

Version for 4 rows:

Row 1: Knit.

Row 2: Purl.

Row 3: Purl.

Row 4: Knit.

Repeat these four rows.

CHECKERBOARD AND WELT STITCH VARIATION

This stitch, based on the 2/2 checkerboard stitch and the welt stitch over 4 rows, is knitted over stitches in multiples of 56. The central panel is made up of 32 stitches in the 2/2 checkerboard stitch (see page 74). It is framed on the edges by the welt stitch over 4 rows of 12 stitches (see above).

The welt stitch can be cast on for the width of the piece, either at the beginning, as shown, or at the end.

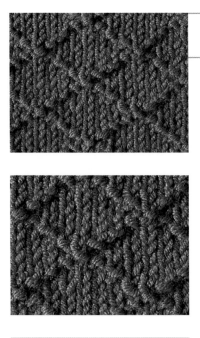

NOTE

By starting with the 8 stitch repeat, you will see that by adjusting the math you can create diamonds of differing sizes.

DIAMOND STITCH

The diamond stitch is made by placing a diagonal line made up of seed stitch on a background of stockinette stitch, forming uniform and evenly spaced diamonds. The number of stitches must be in multiple of 8 with selvage stitches at the beginning and end of the row.

Row 1: 1 selvage st, *P 1 st, K 7 sts*; repeat from * to *; end 1 selvage st.

Row 2: 1 selvage st, *K 1 st, P 5 sts, K 1 st, P 1 st*; repeat from * to *; end 1 selvage st.

Row 3: 1 selvage st, *K 2 sts, P 1 st, K 3 sts, P 1 st, K 1 st*; repeat from * to *; end 1 selvage st.

Row 4: 1 selvage st, *P 2 sts, K 1 st, P 1 st, K 1 st, P 3 sts*; repeat from * to *; end 1 selvage st.

Row 5: 1 selvage st, *K 4 sts, P 1 st, K 3 sts*; repeat from * to *; end 1 selvage st.

Row 6: 1 selvage st, *P 2 sts, K 1 st, P 1 st, K 1 st, P 3 sts*; repeat from * to *; end 1 selvage st.

Row 7: 1 selvage st, *K 2 sts, P 1 st, K 3 sts, P 1 st, K 1 st*; repeat from * to *; end 1 selvage st.

Row 8: 1 selvage st, *K 1 st, P 5 sts, K 1 st, P 1 st*; repeat from * to *; end 1 selvage st.

Repeat these 8 rows.

THE ZIGZAG STITCH

This is a very commonly used stitch in Aran knitting. It forms a uniform zigzag made by seed stitch on a background of stockinette stitch. It is frequently framed by 2 reverse stockinette stitches at the beginning and the end of the pattern. It may be used alone or integrated into a selection of different stitches and motifs.

It is knitted in a multiple of 11 plus 2 reverse stockinette stitches at each end for the swatch.

Row 1: P 2 sts, *P 1 st, K 10 sts*; repeat from * to *; end P 2 sts.

Row 2: K 2 sts, *P 9 sts, K 1 st, P 1 st *; repeat from * to *; end K 2 sts.

Row 3: P 2 sts, *K 2 sts, P 1 st, K 8 sts*; repeat from * to *; end P 2 sts.

Row 4: K 2 sts, *P 7 sts, K 1 st, P 3 sts*; repeat from * to *; end K 2 sts.

Row 5: P 2 sts, *K 2 sts, P 1 st, K 6 sts*; repeat from * to *; end P 2 sts.

Row 6: K 2 sts, *P 5 sts, P 1 st, K 6 sts*; repeat from * to *; end P 2 sts.

Row 7: P 2 sts, K 6 sts, P 1 st, K 4 sts*; repeat from * to *; end P 2 sts.

Row 8: K 2 sts, *P 3 sts, K 1 st, P 7 sts*; repeat from * to *; end K 2 sts.

Row 9: P 2 sts, *K 8 sts, P 1 st, K 2 sts*; repeat from * to *; end P 2 sts.

Row 10: K 2 sts, *P 1 st, K 1 st, P 9 sts*; repeat from * to *; end P 2 sts.

Row 11: P 2 sts, *K 10 sts, P 1 st*; repeat from * to *; end P 2 sts.

This first part of the zigzag slants to the left. Then work backward, that is, start with row 10 and work back to row 2 to slant the second part of the diamond to the right. Begin again with row 1, slanting the zigzag again to the left.

THE PENNANT STITCH

Like the other stitches in this section, this one is made up of alternating knit and purl stitches which form a pattern. It is worked over multiple of 9 stitches plus 1 selvage stitch at each end of the row.

Row 1: 1 selvage st, *K 8 sts, P 1 st*; repeat from * to *; end 1 selvage st.

Row 2: 1 selvage st, *K 2 sts, P 7 sts*; repeat from * to *; end 1 selvage st.

Row 3: 1 selvage st, *K 6 sts, P 3 sts*; repeat from * to *; end 1 selvage st.

Row 4: 1 selvage st, *K 4 sts, P 5 sts*; repeat from * to *; end 1 selvage st.

Row 5: Repeat row 4.

Row 6: Repeat row 3.

Row 7: Repeat row 2.

Row 8: Repeat row 1.

Repeat these 8 rows.

Two Caps and a Beret

ECRU CAP

Size:
3–6 months

Materials:
1-3/4 oz (50 g) of sport weight yarn in the color of your choice Pair size 3 (3-1/4 mm) needles, tapestry needle

Stitch used:
Garter stitch: K every row.

Gauge swatch:
24 sts and 44 rows = 4" (10 cm) in garter stitch using size 3 (3-1/4 mm) needles.

ECRU CAP IN GARTER STITCH

INSTRUCTIONS

Cast on 82 sts. K 5" (13 cm) in garter stitch, then dec 10 sts across the row as follows: 1 selvage stitch, *K 6 sts, K 2 tog*; rep from * to * 10 times, 1 selvage stitch.

Rep this dec row every 4th row a total of 6 times, having 1 st fewer between the decs each time, (12 sts). Cut yarn leaving a long end to sew seam. Thread rem 12 sts onto needle; pull tight and secure. Sew seam. Turn up lower edge for cuff.

TIP

To make a larger cap, cast on 8 stitches more and decrease 11 times across each dec row. To make a smaller cap, cast on 8 stitches fewer and decrease 9 times across each dec row.

POINTED CAP WITH POMPON

Size:
12–18 months

Materials:
3-1/2 oz (100 g) sport weight yarn in the color of your choice
Pair size 3 (3-1/4 mm) needles, tapestry needle

Stitch used:
Stockinette stitch: K 1 row, P 1 row

Gauge swatch:
24 sts and 22 rows = 4" (10 cm) in St st.

BERET WITH POMPON

Size:
12–18 months

Materials:
3-1/2 oz (100 g) DK or light worsted in the color of your choice
One pair each sizes 3 and 6 (3-1/2 mm and 4-1/4 mm) needles

Stitches used:
1/1 rib: K 1, P 1
Seed stitch: Row 1: (K 1, P 1) across.
Row 2: P over the K sts, K over the P sts. Rep these 2 rows for pattern (see also page 72).

Gauge swatch:
With larger needles, 20 sts and 32 rows = 4" (10 cm)

POINTED STOCKINETTE STITCH CAP WITH POMPON

INSTRUCTIONS

Cast on 102 sts. K 6" (165 cm) in St st, then dec 10 sts across the next row as follows: 1 selvage st, * k8 sts, K 2 tog*; rep from * to * 10 times, 1 selvage stitch.

Rep this dec row every 4th row, having 1 st fewer between decs, a total of 9 times, (12 sts). Cut yarn leaving a long end to sew seam. Thread rem 12 sts onto needle; pull tight and secure. Sew seam.

FINISHING TOUCHES

Make a pompon (see page 184) and attach it to the top of the hat. Allow lower edge to curl.

SEED STITCH BERET WITH POMPON

INSTRUCTIONS

With smaller needles, cast on 91 sts and work 12 rows in 1/1 rib, inc 37 sts evenly spaced on the last row. You will have 128 stitches.

Switch to larger needles and work in seed st for 3" (8 cm), then work 12 dec as follows: 1 selvage stitch, *18 seed stitches, work 3 stitches together in pattern*; repeat from * to * 6 times in total, 1 selvage stitch.

Rep dec every 2 rows, 8 more times having 2 sts fewer between the dec each time.

Cut yarn leaving a long end to sew seam. Thread rem 20 sts onto needle; pull tight and secure. Sew seam.

FINISHING TOUCHES

Make a pompon (see page 184) and attach it to the top of the beret.

Toddler's Tricolor Cardigan

CARDIGAN

Size:
2–3 years

Materials:
Worsted weight yarn
5-1/2 oz (150 g) of color A (front and back)
4 oz (100 g) color B (sleeves)
2 oz (50 g) color C (collar)
Pair each size 3 (3-1/4 mm) and 6 (4-1/4 mm) needles
5 coordinating buttons, 5/8" (1.5 cm) in diameter

Stitches used:
Seed stitch: Row 1: (K1, P1) across.
Row 2: P over the K, K over the P.
Garter stitch: K every row.

Gauge Swatch:
With larger needles, 18 sts and 32 rows = 4" (10 cm) in seed st.

INSTRUCTIONS

BACK
With larger needles and color A, cast on 66 sts and work in seed st for 13-1/2" (34 cm).

LEFT FRONT
With larger needles and color A, cast on 37 sts. Knit 30 sts in seed st and 7 sts in garter st for front border.

When piece measures 12" (30 cm), bind off at neck edge 11 sts. Then bind off 3 sts every other row twice. When front is same length as back, bind off rem 20 sts.

Mark for 5 buttons, having the first 1" (2.5 cm) from the lower edge and the last 1/2" (1 cm) from the neck edge.

RIGHT FRONT
Work same as left reversing shaping and working buttonholes as follows: K 3, K 2 tog, yo, K 3 to match the button markers.

SLEEVES
NOTE: The sleeves are worked from the top down.

Sew the shoulder seams. With larger needles, and using color B, pick up the 30 stitches on the front and back on each side of the shoulder seam, adding 1 st for the seam, (61 sts).

Work in seed st and, keeping continuity of pattern, dec 1 st each side every 6 rows 2 times, then every 8 rows 8 times, (41 sts).

At 11" (28 cm) from beg, bind off all sts in pattern.

FINISHING TOUCHES

Block lightly. Sew side and sleeve seams.

For the collar, with smaller needles and color C, pick up the 16 stitches of the right front neck edge, beginning at the middle of the button band, then the 26 stitches of the back and the 16 stitches on the left front up to the middle of the button band. Work 3-1/2" (9 cm) in seed st. Bind off.

Sew the buttons on the button band opposite the buttonholes.

Ribbed Stitches

These are most often found at the base of knits to pull in at the waist, hips, and wrists. They are knitted with needles 2 sizes smaller than those used for the body of the work.

You should keep an even tension because the yarn goes back and forth between the stitches: ribs that are too loose lose their purpose. Note that 1/1 ribs do a better job of pulling in than 2/2 ribs.

Many types of ribs are used for the whole of "close fitting" knits, socks, hats, scarves, headbands, and afghans working with many different stitches.

1/1 RIB STITCH

Row 1: *K 1 st, P 1 st*; repeat from * to * across.
Row 2: Work the stitches as in row 1, K over the K sts; P over the P sts.
Rep these 2 rows as often as needed.

TIP

Casting on an uneven number of stitches means that the first and last stitch will look the same, and you will be able to tell the right side from the wrong side.

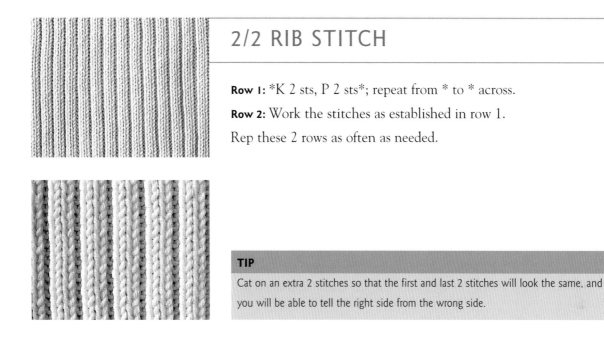

2/2 RIB STITCH

Row 1: *K 2 sts, P 2 sts*; repeat from * to * across.

Row 2: Work the stitches as established in row 1.

Rep these 2 rows as often as needed.

TIP

Cat on an extra 2 stitches so that the first and last 2 stitches will look the same, and you will be able to tell the right side from the wrong side.

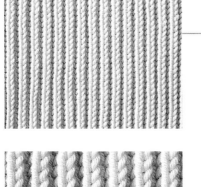

ENGLISH RIB STITCH

This stitch gives the appearance of a rib stitch without purling. It doesn't pull in as much as a true rib. The number of stitches must be uneven plus 1 selvage stitch on each side.

Row 1: 1 selvage st, K all sts, 1 selvage st.

Row 2: 1 selvage st, *K 1 st, K into the st from the row below*, repeat from * to *; end K 1 st, 1 selvage st.

Row 3: 1 selvage st, *K into the st from the row below, K 1 st*; repeat from * to *; end K 1 st, 1 selvage st.

Repeat rows 2 and 3.

Knit into the row below: Insert your right needle through the center of the stitch on the preceding row and knit it, letting the upper stitch unravel.

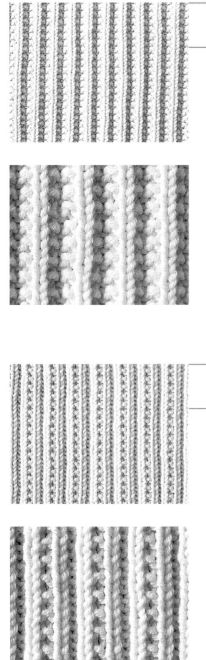

MOCK ENGLISH RIB STITCH

The number of stitches must be multiple of 4, plus 3, plus 1 selvage stitch on each side.

Row 1: 1 selvage st, *K 3 sts, P 1 st*; repeat from * to *; end K 3 sts, 1 selvage st.

Row 2: 1 selvage st, *K 1 st, P 1 st, K 2 sts*; repeat from * to *; end K 1 st, P 1 st, K 1 st, 1 selvage st.

Repeat these two rows.

BEADED RIB STITCH

The number of stitches must be a multiple of 5, plus 2.

Row 1: *P 2 sts, K 1 st, P 1 st, K 1 st*; repeat from * to *; end P 2 sts.

Row 2: *K 2 sts, P 3 sts*; repeat from * to *; end K 2 sts.

Repeat these two rows.

This stitch may also be used on the reverse side, as shown in the photos below.

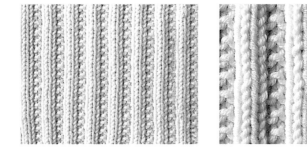

7/3 FLAT RIB STITCH

The number of stitches must be in multiple of 10, plus 7.

Row 1: K 7 sts, *P 3 sts, K 7 sts*; repeat from * to * across.
Row 2: P 7 sts, *K 3 sts, P 7 sts*; repeat from * to * across.
Repeat these two rows.

9/9 FLAT RIB STITCH

The number of stitches must be in multiple of 18, plus 9.

Row 1: K 9 sts, *P 9 sts, K 9 sts*; repeat from * to * across.
Row 2: P 9 sts, *K 9 sts, P 9 sts*; repeat from * to * across.
Repeat these two rows.

FANCY RIB STITCH

The number of stitches must be in multiple of 6, plus 3.

Row 1: P 1 st, K 1 st, P 1 st, *K 3 sts, P 1 st, K 1 st, P 1 st*; repeat from * to * across.

Row 2: P 1 st, *K 1 st, P 5 sts*; repeat from * to *; end K 1 st, P 1 st.

Repeat these two rows.

Women's Sweater in 9/9 Rib Stitch

SWEATER

Size:
Large

Materials:
Anny Blatt Merino Wool
(50g/125m balls), 700 g or 25 oz
in the color of your choice.
One pair each sizes 3 and 4 (3-1/4
and 3.5 mm) needles

Stitches used:
3/3 rib: K 3 sts, P 3 sts.
9/9 rib: K 9 sts, P 9 sts.

Gauge swatch:
With larger needles working in pattern
stitch; 27 sts and 34 rows = 4" (10 cm)

INSTRUCTIONS

BACK

With smaller needles cast on 153 sts and work 4" (10 cm) in 3/3 rib, beginning with P 3 sts.

With larger needles, continue in 9/9 rib stitch beginning with P 9 sts.

Work even in pattern until piece measures 23-1/4" (59 cm). Begin the neck shaping and the shoulder shaping on the next row. Bind off 18 sts at the beg of the next 6 rows, (45 sts) and at the same time, bind off the center 35 sts, and working each side separately, bind off 3 sts at each neck edge, then 2 sts once.

FRONT

Work same as back until pieces measures 21-1/4" (54 cm). Bind off the center 15 sts for the neck shaping, then working each side separately bind off 4 sts at each neck edge once, 3 sts once, 2 sts twice. Dec 1 st at neck edge 4 times and when piece measures same as back, bind off same as back.

SLEEVES

With smaller needles cast on 87 sts and work 4" (10 cm) in 3/3 rib, beginning and ending with 3 knit stitches.

With larger needles, work in 9/9 rib, beginning with 3 knit sts, then repeating 9 purl sts, 9 knit sts to finish with 3 knit sts.

Keeping continuity of pattern, inc 1 st each side every 6th row 18 times, (123 sts).

When piece measures 17" (43 cm), bind off all sts.

FINISHING TOUCHES

Block the pieces lightly on the wrong side.

Sew the left shoulder. With smaller needles, pick up the 45 stitches from the back of the neck, then 34 stitches on the front side, the 15 on the center front, and the 34 on the second side. On the 128 stitches, work 6-1/4" (16 cm) in 3/3 rib stitch with 1 selvage stitch on each side, then bind off all the stitches in ribbing using the larger needle.

Sew the right shoulder and the neck, reversing the direction of the sewing halfway to hide the seam when the collar is turned down. Sew the sleeves to the sweater, then seam them and the sides of the sweater.

NOTE

The stitches in the collar may be picked up using a set of four needles or with a circular needle, as long as they are number 3 in size. In this case, reduce two stitches to the total number to obtain a multiple of 6. The neck will be knitted around using the 3/3 rib stitch. This sophisticated technique means you do not need to sew the neck.

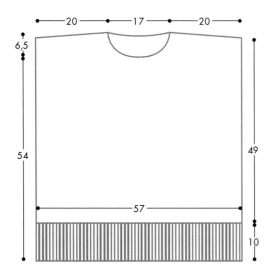

Front and back (in centimeters)

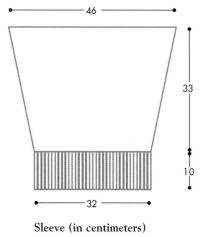

Sleeve (in centimeters)

Men's or Women's Scarf in 2/2 Rib Stitch

SCARF

Dimensions:
Woman's scarf: 11" x 63" (28 cm x 160 cm)
Man's scarf: 11" x 86" (28 cm x 220 cm)

Materials:
Sport weight yarn:
18 oz (500 g) for woman's
25 oz (700 g) for man's
Pair size 3 (3-1/4 mm) needles

Stitches used:
2/2 rib: K 2 sts, P 2 sts.

Gauge swatch:
36 sts and 30 rows (unstretched) = 4" (10 cm).

INSTRUCTIONS

WOMAN'S SCARF
Cast on 106 sts and work 63" (170 cm) in 2/2 rib.
Then bind off all the stitches evenly in ribbing pattern.

MAN'S SCARF
Cast on 106 sts and work 86" (220 cm) in 2/2 rib.
Then bind off all the stitches evenly in ribbing pattern.

FINISHING TOUCHES

Block lightly.

Scarf or Stole in Fancy Rib Stitch

SCARF / STOLE

Dimensions:
Stole: 21-1/2" x 79" (55 cm x 200 cm)
Scarf: 12-1/2" x 63" (32 cm x 160 cm)

Materials:
Bouton D'Or Croisière Superwash (50g/125m balls) 600 g or 22 oz for the stole
400 grams or 14 oz for the scarf
Pair size 3 (3-1/4 mm) needles

Stitch used:
Fancy rib stitch (see page 88)

Gauge swatch:
Working in fancy rib pattern, 20 sts and 28 rows = 4" (10 cm).

INSTRUCTIONS

STOLE

Cast 111 stitches on the needles and knit using the fancy rib stitch in the following manner:

Row 1: * 1 purl stitch, 1 knit stitch, 1 purl stitch, 3 knit stitches *, repeat from * to *, then finish the row with 1 purl stitch, 1 knit stitch, 1 purl stitch.
Row 2: 1 purl stitch, *1 knit stitch, 5 purl stitches *; repeat from * to *; end 1 knit stitch, 1 purl stitch.
Repeat these 2 rows.

At 79" (200 cm) in total length, bind off all the stitches in pattern.

SCARF

Cast 63 stitches on the needles and knit 63" (160) centimeters in fancy rib stitch. Bind off in pattern.

FINISHING TOUCHES

Block lightly.

Small Angora Lap Blanket in English Rib Stitch

SMALL LAP BLANKET

Dimensions:
25-1/2" x 63" (65 x 160 cm)

Materials:
Anny Blatt Supreme Angora
(10g/25 m balls), 11 oz (300 g) in
the color of your choice.
Pair size 8 (5 mm) needles

Stitches used:
English rib stitch (see page 85)

Gauge Swatch:
Working in English rib stitch, 16
sts and 30 rows = 4" (10 cm).

NOTE

This lap blanket may also be
made with 500 grams of 70%
Angora worked double with
number 6 needles. The gauge
swatch would then be 14 stitches
and 28 rows.

INSTRUCTIONS

Cast 105 stitches. Knit the English rib stitch in the following manner:

Row 1: Knit all stitches.
Row 2: 1 selvage stitch, *K 1 st, 1 double stitch (insert your needle in the center stitch on the preceding row and knit the stitch, dropping the stitch above)*; repeat from * to *; end 1 knit stitch, 1 selvage stitch.
Row 3: 1 selvage stitch, *1 double stitch, 1 knit stitch*; repeat from * to *; end 1 double stitch, 1 selvage stitch.
Repeat rows 2 and 3.

At 63" (160 cm) in total length, bind off all the stitches in ribbing.

FINISHING TOUCHES

Lightly steam iron the finished lap blanket on the back.

Cable Stitches

Cables are knitting stitches that change places. They are ususally surrounded by reverse stock-inette stitch, which sets them off. They are worked with a double pointed needle or a special cable needle with a center bend or a J bend. Cable stitches may be used in multiple ways, to give a pattern a regional look or to follow the newest fashions.

BASIC TECHNIQUES AND PRINCIPLES

The techniques used to make the various cables are simple but require attention and precision. The basic principles are frequently repeated over and over in patterns. The stitches cross either in front or in back of the work, which causes them to tilt to the left or right.

CABLES CROSSING TO THE LEFT

1 and 2: Slip the required number of stitches on a double-pointed needle or cable needle and hold in front of the work.
3. Knit the required number of stitches from the left needle.
4. Then knit the held stitches from the cable needle.

CABLES CROSSING TO THE RIGHT

1 and 2: Slip the required number of stitches on a double-pointed needle or on a cable needle, and held in back of the work.

3: Knit the required number of stitches from the left needle.

4: Then knit the held stitches from the cable needle.

NOTE

It is important to make a separate swatch for each cable. Because of the raised stitches caused by the twisting of the cable, the work will tighten noticeably. Therefore the gauge swatch for a cabled pattern will have a larger number of stitches than one worked in flat stockinette stitch.

For classic cable stitches, the cabled stitches between the two columns of reverse stockinette (or perhaps a larger background of reverse stockinette) are always crossed in the same direction, usually every six to twelve rows.

BASIC CABLE STITCH

The number of stitches must be in multiples of 2 and 6, plus 2.

Row 1 and 3: P 2 sts, *K 4 sts, P 2 sts*; repeat from * to * across.

Rows 2, 4, 6: Work the stitches as established above.

Row 5: P 2 stitches, *slip 2 stitches on a cable needle held to the front of the work, knit the remaining 2 cable stitches on the left needle, then knit the 2 slipped stitches on the cable needle, work 2 purl stitches*; repeat from * to * across.

Repeat these 6 rows.

> **NOTE**
>
> Basic cables are generally worked with the cable stitches divided in half. That is, 4 stitches becomes 2 stitches worked before the other 2 stitches; 6 stitches becomes 3 stitches worked before the other 3 stitches, etc.

CABLE AND RIB PATTERN

The number of stitches must be in multiples of 20, plus 2.

Row 1: K 2 sts, *P 2 sts, K 4 sts, P 2 sts, K 2 sts, P 2 sts, K 4 sts, P 2 sts, K 2 sts*; repeat from * to * across.

Rows 2 and all even rows: Work the stitches as established, keeping the knits over the knits and the purls over the purls.

Row 5: K 2 sts, *P 2 sts, slip the next 2 sts onto a cable needle and hold in back, K the next 2 sts, then K the 2 sts from the cable needle, P 2 sts, slip the next 2 sts onto a cable needle and hold in front, K the next 2 sts, then K the 2 sts from the cable needle, P 2 sts, K 2 sts*; repeat from * to * across.

Row 6: Repeat row 2.

Repeat from rows 3 through 6.

CORDED CABLE

It is knitted over 6 stitches with 3 purl stitches on either side.

Row 1: P 3 sts, *K 6 sts, P 3 sts*; repeat from * to * across.

Rows 2 and all even rows: Work the stitches as established above.

Row 3: Repeat row 1.

Row 5: P 3 sts, *Slip 3 stitches onto a cable needle and hold in back, knit the next 3 stitches from the left needle, then the 3 stitches from the cable needle, P 3 sts*; repeat from * to * across.
Repeat these 6 rows.

BRAIDED CABLE

This stitch is knitted over 9 stitches with 3 purl stitches on either side.

Row 1: P 3 sts, *K 9 sts, P 3 sts*; repeat from * to * across.

Row 2 and all even rows: Work the stitches as established above.

Row 3: P 3 sts, *Slip 3 stitches onto a cable needle and hold in back, K 3, knit the 3 stitches from the cable needle, then knit the next 3 stitches from the left needle, P 3*; repeat from * to * across.

Row 5: P 3 sts, *K 3 sts, slip 3 stitches onto a cable needle placed in front of work, knit the next 3 stitches, then knit the 3 stitches on the cable needle, P 3 sts*; repeat from * to * across.
Repeat rows 3 to 6.

This cable forms a very tight braid.

WOVEN CABLE STITCH

This cable is worked over 18 stitches with 5 purl stitches on each side.

Row 1: P 5 sts, K 18 sts, P 5 sts.

Row 2 and all even rows: Work the stitches as established above.

Row 3: P 5 sts, *slip 3 st on a cable needle and hold in back, K the next 3 sts from the left needle and then the 3 from the cable needle*; repeat from * to * two more times; P 5 sts.

Row 5: P 5 sts, K 18 sts, P 5 sts.

Row 7: P 5 sts, K 3 sts, *slip 3 sts onto a cable needle and hold in front, K the next 3 sts from the left needle, then the 3 on the cable needle*; repeat from * to * one more time; K 3 sts, P 5 sts.

Repeat these 8 rows.

DOUBLE CABLE STITCH

Also called "the horseshoe stitch," the double cable stitch is 12 sts with 4 purl sts on each side. The number of sts is a multiple of 16, plus 4.

Row 1: P 4 sts, *K 12 sts , P 4 sts*; repeat from * to * across.

Row 2 and all even rows: Work all sts as established.

Row 3: Repeat row 1.

Row 5: P 4 sts, *slip next 3 sts to cable needle and hold in back, K next 3 sts from left needle and then the 3 sts from cable needle, slip next 3 sts to cable needle and hold in front, K next 3 sts from left needle and the 3 sts from cable needle, P 4 sts*; repeat from * to * across.

Rows 7, 9, and 11: Repeat row 1.

Row 12: Repeat row 12.

Row 13: Repeat rows 5 through 12 for pattern.

CROSSED CABLES ON A BASE OF 2/2 RIB STITCH

This cable is worked over multiple of 8, plus 2.

Row 1: P 2 sts, *K 2 sts, P 2 sts, K 2 sts, P 2 sts*; rep from * to * across.
Row 2 and all even rows: Work the stitches as established above.
Rows 3 and 5: Repeat row 1.
Row 7: P 2 sts, *slip 3 sts onto a cable needle and hold in front, K the next 3 sts from the left needle, then the 3 on the cable needle, P 2 sts*; repeat from * to * across.
Repeat these 8 rows.

Taking into account the thickness of the yarn and the size of the needles, you may want to make a more elongated cable, crossing the stitches every 10 or 12 rows.

CABLES ON A BACKGROUND OF SEED STITCH

This cable is worked over multiple of 22, plus 12.

Row 1: *Work 12 seed sts, K 10 sts*; repeat from * to *; end 12 seed sts.
Row 2 and all even rows: Work the stitches as established above.
Rows 3 and 5: Repeat row 1.
Row 7: *Work 12 seed sts, K 1 st, slip 4 sts onto a cable needle and hold in back and K the next 4 sts and then the 4 on the cable needle, K 1 st*; repeat from * to *; end 12 seed stitches.
Repeat these 8 rows.

NOTE
You will find that the spectrum of cable stitches is infinite, each with its own personality.

Each cable is bordered by a knit stitch, which allows you to mark clearly the boundaries of the seed stitch.

HIGH RELIEF CABLE ON REVERSE STOCKINETTE

This cable crosses at close intervals to accentuate the raised quality, either on a background of reverse stockinette or seed stitch.
Cast 12 stitches and 1 selvage stitch on each side for the sample.

Rows 1, 3, and 5: 1 selvage st, K 12 sts, 1 selvage st.

Rows 2 and all even rows: Work the stitches as established above.

Row 7: 1 selvage st, slip 6 sts onto a cable needle and hold in back, K the next 6 sts from the left needle, then the 6 on the cable needle, 1 selvage st.

Repeat these 8 rows.

THE WAVE STITCH

These cables, whose stitches cross next to each other, form waves that look like the movement of sand on dunes or water in a river. The number of stitches is a multiple of 12, plus 1 selvage stitch on each side of the sample.

Row 1: 1 selvage st, K 12 sts, 1 selvage st.

Rows 2 and all even rows: 1 selvage st, P 12 sts, 1 selvage st.

Row 3: 1 selvage st, slip 3 sts onto a cable needle and hold in front, K the next 3 sts and then the 3 stitches from the cable needle, K 6 sts, 1 selvage st.

Row 5: Repeat row 1.

Row 7: 1 selvage st, K 6 sts, slip 3 sts onto a cable needle and hold in back, K 3 sts, K the 3 sts from the cable needle *, 1 selvage st.

Repeat these 8 rows.

Toddler's Cable Sweater

SWEATER

Size:
12–18 months

Materials:
7 oz (200 g) light sport yarn in the color of your choice
One pair each size 0 (2 mm) and 3 (3-1/4 mm) needles
Cable needle
3 small buttons

Stitches used:
2/2 rib: K 2 sts, P 2 sts.
Garter stitch: K every row.
Seed stitch: K 1 st and P 1 st alternated every row.
Right cable stitch, 8 stitches and 8 rows

Gauge swatch:
On larger needle 26 sts and 34 rows = 4" (10 cm)

INSTRUCTIONS

BACK

With smaller needles, cast on 74 sts and work 1-1/2" (4 cm) in 2/2 rib.

Change to larger needles. On next row, work 1 selvage st, *8 seed stitches, K 8 sts*; repeat from * to * 3 times more, then work 8 seed sts, 1 selvage st for first cable pattern row.

For pattern, work cables as follows:

Rows 1, 3 and 7: K 8 sts.
Rows 2 and all even rows: P 8 sts.
Row 5: Slip 4 sts to a cable needle and hold in back, K next 4 sts from left needle, then K 4 sts from cable needle.
Repeat these 8 rows for cable pattern.

Work in seed st and cable pattern (starting now with a Row 2) until piece measures 12-1/2" (32 cm) from beg.

Bind off 20 sts for the right shoulder, then knit the next 34 for the neck and place on holder, then with the smaller needle, work 6 rows of garter stitch on the rem 20 sts for the button placket.

Bind off the stitches of the button placket.

FRONT

Work as for back until the piece measures 11" (28 cm), place the center 12 sts on a holder for the neck and working on the 31 sts only of the left side, bind off 3 sts at the neck edge, then 2 sts 2 times and dec 1 st 4 times. When piece measures same as back, bind off rem 20 sts. Work right side the same, rev shaping and at the same time, when piece measures 11-3/4" (30 cm) work as follows: Change to smaller needles and work buttonhole band. Work 4 rows of garter st. On the 5th row, K 1, K 2 tog, yo, K 6, K 2 tog, yo, K 6, K 2 tog, yo, K 1. K 5 more rows. Bind off.

SLEEVES

With small needles, cast on 50 sts and work in 2/2 rib for 1-1/2"
(4 cm). Change to larger needles, work *8 seed sts, K 2, inc, K 2,
inc, K 2*; rep from * to * 2 times more; end 8 seed sts, (56 sts).
Work seed st and 8-row cables the same as for the back and front
and inc 1 st each side every 8th row 8 times, keeping continuity
of pattern.

When piece measures 9-1/2" (24 cm), bind off all sts.

FINISHING TOUCHES

Block lightly.

Sew the right shoulder. With smaller needles, pick up 18 sts on
the right side of the front neck edge, then pick up the 12 sts from
the center, 18 on the second side, 34 on the back neck edge, and 6
on the button placket. Work in 2/2 rib for 1" (2.5 cm). Bind off in
ribbing. Overlap the 2 halves of the button placket; pin layers
together. Mark side edges 5-1/2" (14 cm) below shoulders. Sew
sleeves in place between markers. Sew sleeve and side seams. Sew
on the buttons.

Natural Wool Sweater in Wave Stitch

THE SWEATER

Size:
Medium

Materials:
Anny Blatt Rustic wool (50 g/58 m balls), 31-1/2 oz (850 g) in the color of your choice
Pair each size 8 (5 mm) and 10 (6 mm)
Cable needle

Stitches used:
1/1 cable rib stitch
Wave stitch (see page 104)

Gauge Swatch:
Working in wave stitch on larger needles, 20 sts and 18 rows = 4" (10 cm).

INSTRUCTIONS

BACK

Cast 99 stitches on smaller needles. Work English rib stitch for 4" (10 cm).

With larger needles, work Row 1 of the wave stitch (knit across) with 1 selvage stitch on each side and making 11 increases evenly spaced across the first row: you will obtain 110 stitches.

Rows 1 and 5: Knit.
Rows 2, 4, 6, and 8: Purl.
Row 3: *Slip 3 sts on a cable needle and hold in front of the work, K the next 3 sts and then the 3 sts on the cable needle, P 6 sts*; repeat from * to *.
Row 7: *K 6 sts, slip 3 on a cable needle and hold in back of work, K the next 3 sts and then the 3 sts on the cable needle*; repeat from * to *.
Repeat these 8 rows.

Starting now with a row 2, continue in pattern until piece is 21-1/4" (54 cm). Begin shaping shoulders and neck at the same time as follows: On each shoulder edge, bind off 13 sts once, then 12 sts once and place the center 24 sts on a holder for neck. Working each side separately, bind off 5 sts at each neck edge once.

FRONT

Begin as you did for the back. When piece measures 18-1/2" (47 cm) in length, place the center 10 stitches on a holder for the neck, then finish each side separately, binding off every other row at neck edge, then 3 sts once, 2 sts 3 times, and 1 st 3 times.

At 54 cm in total height, cast off the shoulders as you did for the back.

SLEEVES

Cast 45 stitches on smaller needles. Work 4" (10 cm) in English rib stitch.

With larger needles, work row 1 of wave stitch, with 1 selvage st each side and working 13 increases evenly spaced, (58 sts).

Continuing in wave stitch pattern, increase 1 st at each side every 2 rows 5 times, then every 4 rows 12 times, keeping continuity of pattern, then work even on 92 sts.

At 18-1/2" (47 cm) in total length, bind off all sts.

FINISHING TOUCHES

After pinning all the pieces on the back, lightly steam-iron them with a damp cloth.

Sew the left shoulder. With smaller needles, pick up the 34 sts on the back neck, 21 sts on left front, 14 sts from front holder, 21 sts on right front, (90 sts). Work 3" (8 cm) in English rib, then bind off in ribbing.

Sew the right shoulder and the edge of the neckband. Mark side edges 9" (23 cm) below shoulder seams. Attach the sleeves between the markers. Seam sleeves and sides of sweater.

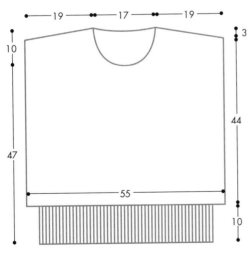

Front and back (in centimeters)

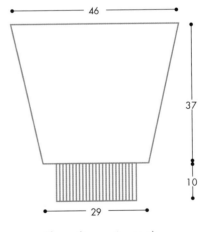

Sleeve (in centimeters)

Aran Stitches

Aran stitches are most often used in combination of cable stitches, crossed stitches, twisted stitches, knots, waving movements, and diamonds, made with great precision on natural, plain worsted weight wool.

It is on the Aran Islands, situated to the west of Ireland, where women have created sweaters, hand-knitted of high-quality, usually with their natural lanolin intact, wool furnished by the many herds of sheep which populate the islands. They knew how to embellish their knitting with numerous motifs: Celtic symbols, crosses, diamonds, zigzags, etc. We also find, since the sixteenth century, the influence of central Europe. Religion inspired the naming of these different stitches, such as the Trinity stitch, the tree of life, and Jacob's ladder, which have been passed down from generation to generation all the way to today.

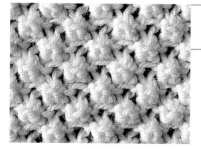

THE TRINITY STITCH

The number of stitches is a multiple of 4, plus 1 selvage stitch on each side for the swatch.

Row 1: 1 selvage st, *K 1, P 1, and K 1 all in the first st, P 3 tog*; repeat from * to *; end 1 selvage st.
Row 2: Purl.
Row 3: 1 selvage st, *P 3 tog, K 1, P 1 and K 1 all in the next st*; repeat from * to *; end 1 selvage st.
Row 4: Purl.
Repeat these 4 rows.

THE HONEYCOMB STITCH

The number of stitches is a multiple of 8, plus 1 selvage stitch on each side for the swatch.

Row 1: 1 selvage st, *P 2, K 4, P 2*; repeat from * to *; end 1 selvage st.

Rows 2, 4, 6, and 8: Work the stitches as established.

Row 3: 1 selvage st, *slip 2 sts onto a cable needle and hold at back of work, K 2 sts, then P the 2 on the cable needle, slip 2 sts onto a cable needle and hold at front of work, P 2 sts, then K the 2 sts on the cable needle*; repeat from * to *; end 1 selvage st.

Row 5: 1 selvage st, *K 2 sts, P 2 sts, K 2 sts*; repeat from * to *; end 1 selvage st.

Row 7: 1 selvage st, *slip 2 sts onto a cable needle and hold at front of work, P 2 sts, then K the 2 on the cable needle, slip 2 sts onto a cable needle and hold at back of work, K 2 sts, then P the 2 sts on the cable needle*; repeat from * to *; end 1 selvage stitch.

Repeat these 8 rows.

THE TREE OF LIFE STITCH

Each motif is knitted over 16 stitches.

Row 1: P 6 sts, place 1 st on an auxiliary needle behind work, K 1 st, K the stitch on the auxiliary needle, place 1 st on auxiliary needle in front of work, K 1 st, K the st on the auxiliary needle, P 6 sts.

Row 2: K 5 sts, place 1 st on an auxiliary needle and hold in front of work, P 1 st, K the st on the auxiliary needle, P 2 sts, slip 1 st on an auxiliary needle, K 5 sts.

Row 3: P 4 sts, place 1 st onto an auxiliary needle behind work, K 1 st, P the st on the auxiliary needle, place 1 st on an auxiliary needle behind the work, K 1 st, K the st on the auxiliary needle, place 1 st on an auxiliary needle in front of the work, K 1 st, K the st on the auxiliary needle, place 1 st on an auxiliary needle in front of the work, P 1 st, K the st on the auxiliary needle, P 4 sts.

Row 4: K 3 sts, place 1 st on an auxiliary needle in front of the work, P 1 st, K the st on the auxiliary needle, K 1 st, P 4 sts, K 1 st, place 1 st on an auxiliary needle behind the work, K 1 st, P the st on the auxiliary needle, K 3 sts.

Row 5: P 2 sts, place 1 st on an auxiliary needle behind the work, K 1 st, P the st on the auxiliary needle, P 1 st, place 1 st on an auxiliary needle behind the work, K 1 st, P the st on the auxiliary needle, K 2 sts, place 1 st on an auxiliary needle in front of the work, P 1 st, K the st on the auxiliary needle, P 1 st, place 1 st on an auxiliary needle in front of the work, P 1 st, K the st on the auxiliary needle, P 2 sts.

Row 6: K 2 sts, P 1 st, K 2 sts, P 1 st, K 1 st, P 2 sts, K 1 st, P 1 st, K 2 sts, P 1 st, K 2 sts.

Row 7: P 2 sts, 1 bobble (work K 1, P 1, K 1, P 1 all in the next st; turn, purl these 4 sts; turn, K these sts; turn, P 2 tog twice; turn, K 2 tog), P 1 st, place 1 st on an auxiliary needle behind the work, K 1 st, P the st on the auxiliary needle, P 1 st, K 2 sts, P 1 st, place 1 st on an auxiliary needle in front of the work, P 1 st, K the st on the auxiliary needle, P 1 st, 1 bobble in the next st, P 2 sts.

Row 8: K 4 sts, P 1 st, K 2 sts, P 2 sts, K 2 sts, P 1 st, K 4 sts.

Row 9: P 4 sts, 1 bobble in the next st, P 2 sts, K 2 sts, P 2 sts, 1 bobble in the next st, P 4 sts.

Row 10: K 7 sts, P 2 sts, K 7 sts. Repeat these 10 rows.

DIAMONDS WITH A DOUBLE MOSS STITCH CENTER

Each pattern is made over 17 stitches.

Row 1: P6, K2, P1, K2, P6.

Row 2 and all even rows: Work the stitches as established.

Row 3: P6, slip the next 3 stitches on an auxiliary needle behind the work, K 2 sts, replace the P st on the auxiliary needle on the left needle and P, K the remaining 2 sts on the auxiliary needle, P 6 sts.

Row 5: P 5 sts, place 1 st on an auxiliary needle behind the work, K 2 sts, P the st on the auxiliary needle, K 1 st, place the next 2 sts on an auxiliary needle in front of the work, P the next st, K the 2 sts on the auxiliary needle, P 5 sts.

Row 7: P 4 sts, place 1 st on an auxiliary needle behind the work, K 2 sts, P stitch on the auxiliary needle, K 1 st, P 1 st, K 1 st, slip 2 sts on an auxiliary needle in front of the work, P 1 st, K the 2 sts on the auxiliary needle, P 4 sts.

Row 9: P 3 sts, place 1 st on an auxiliary needle behind the work, K 2 sts, P the st on the auxiliary needle, K 1 st, P 1 st, K 1 st, P 1 st, K 1 st, place 2 sts on an auxiliary needle in front of the work, P 1 st, K the 2 sts on an auxiliary needle, P 3 sts.

Row 11: P 2 sts, place 1 st on an auxiliary needle behind the work, K 2 sts, P the st on the auxiliary needle, K 1 st, P 1 st, K 1 st, P 1 st, K 1 st, P 1 st, K 1 st, place 2 sts on an auxiliary needle in front of the work, P 1 st, K the 2 sts on the auxiliary needle, P 2 sts.

Row 13: P 2 sts, place 2 sts on an auxiliary needle in front of the work, P 1 st, K the 2 sts on the auxiliary needle, P 1 st, K 1 st, P 1 st, K 1 st, P 1 st, K 1 st, P 1 st, place 1 st on an auxiliary needle behind the work, K 2 sts, P the stitch on an auxiliary needle, P 2 sts.

Row 15: P 3 sts, place 2 sts on an auxiliary needle in front of the work, P 1 st, K the 2 sts on an auxiliary needle, P 1 st, K 1 st, P 1 st, K 1 st, P 1 st, place 1 st on an auxiliary needle behind the work, K 2 sts, P st on auxiliary needle, P 3 sts.

Row 17: P 4 sts, place 2 sts on an auxiliary needle in front of the work, P 1 st, K the 2 sts

on an auxiliary needle, P 1 st, K 1 st, P 1 st, place 1 st on an auxiliary needle behind the work, K 2 sts, P the st on auxiliary needle, P 4 sts.

Row 19: P 5 sts, place 2 sts on an auxiliary needle in front of the work, P 1 st, K the 2 sts on auxiliary needle, P 1 st, place 1 st on an auxiliary needle behind the work, K 2 sts, P st on auxiliary needle, P 5 sts.

Always repeat rows 3 through 20 for pattern.

VARIATION ON A THEME OF CROSSED DIAMONDS

This variation is made up of crossed diamonds with a background in double moss stitch and crossed diamonds with bobbles on reverse stockinette. The pattern is made over 13 stitches plus 2 purl stitches on each side for the swatch.

Row 1: P 6 sts, slip the next 3 sts on an auxiliary needle in front of the work, K 2 sts, replace the P st (st at left) on the auxiliary needle on the left needle and P it, K the remaining 2 pending sts on the auxiliary needle, P 6 sts.

Row 2 and all even rows: Work the sts as indicated above.

Row 3: P 5 sts, place 1 st on an auxiliary needle behind the work, K 2 sts, P the pending st, K 1 st, place the next 2 sts on an auxiliary needle in front of the work, P 1 st, K the 2 pending sts, P 5 sts.

Row 5: P 4 sts, place 1 stitch on an auxiliary needle behind the work, K 2 sts, P the pending st, K 1 st, P 1 st, K 1 st, slip 2 sts on an auxiliary needle in front of the work, P 1 st, K the 2 pending sts, P 4 sts.

Row 7: P 3 sts, place 1 st on an auxiliary needle behind the work, K 2 sts, P the pending st, K 1 st, P 1 st, K 1 st, P 1 st, K 1 st, place 2 sts on an auxiliary needle in front of the work, P 1 st, K the 2 pending sts, P 3 sts.

Row 9: P 2 sts, place 1 st on an auxiliary needle behind the work, K 2 sts, P the pending st, K 1 st, P 1 st, K 1 st, P 1 st, K 1 st, P 1 st, K 1 st, place 2 sts on an auxiliary needle in front of the work, P 1 st, K the 2 pending sts, P 2 sts.

Row 11: P 2 sts, place 2 sts on an auxiliary needle in front of the work, P 1 st, K the 2 pending sts, P 1 st, K 1 st, P 1 st, K 1 st, P 1 st, K 1 st, P 1 st, place 1 st on an auxiliary needle behind the work, K 2 sts, P the pending st, P 2 sts.

Row 13: P 3 sts, place 2 sts on an auxiliary needle in front of the work, P 1 st, K the 2 pending sts, P 1 st, K 1 st, P 1 st, K 1 st, P 1 st, place 1 stitch on an auxiliary needle behind the work, K 1 sts, P the pending st, P 3 sts.

Row 15: P 4 sts, place 2 sts on an auxiliary needle in front of the work, P 1 st, K the 2 pending sts, P 1 st, K 1 st, P 1 st, place 1 st on an auxiliary needle behind the work, K 2 sts, P the pending st, P 4 sts.

Row 17: P 5 sts, place 2 sts on an auxiliary needle in front of the work, P 1 st, K the 2 pending sts, P 1 st, place 1 st on an auxiliary needle behind the work, K 2 sts, P the pending st, P 5 sts.

Row 19: Repeat row 1.

Row 21: P 5 sts, place 1 st on an auxiliary needle behind the work, K 2 sts, P the pending st, P 1 st, place 2 sts on an auxiliary needle in front of the work, P 1 st, K the 2 pending sts, P 5 sts.

Row 23: P 4 sts, place 1 st on an auxiliary needle behind the work, K 2 sts, P the pending st, P 3 sts, place 2 sts on an auxiliary needle in front of the work, P 1 st, K the 2 pending sts, P 4 sts.

Row 25: P 4 sts, K 2 sts, P 2 sts, 1 bobble, P 2 sts, K 2 sts, P 4 sts.

Row 27: P 4 sts, place 2 sts on an auxiliary needle in front of the work, P 1 st, K the 2 pending sts, P 3 sts, place 1 st on an auxiliary needle behind the work, K 2 sts, P the pending st, P 4 sts.

Row 29: P 5 sts, place 2 sts on an auxiliary needle in front of the work, P 1 st, K the 2 pending sts, P 1 st, place 1 st on an auxiliary needle behind the work, K 2 sts, P the pending st, P 5 sts.

Row 30: Repeat row 2.

Repeat rows 1 through 30 for pattern.

CROSSED STITCHES WITHOUT AN AUXILIARY NEEDLE

It is possible to cross stitches without the help of an extra needle. These stitches often accompany cable stitches and Irish motifs. They are most often worked diagonally, in zigzags and/or in diamonds, bordering more important sections of your knitting. They can be adorned with bobbles.

STITCHES CROSSED TO THE RIGHT

1. Work up to the two stitches that are to be crossed.

2. Then with the thread behind the work and, passing in front of the purl stitch, knit the knit stitch without letting it fall from the left needle.

3 and 4. Bring the thread to the front, purl the purl stitch, then let the two stitches fall.

On the next row, work the stitches as now established.

STITCHES CROSSED TO THE LEFT

1. Work up to the two stitches that are to be crossed.

2. Then with the thread in front of the work and, passing behind the knit stitch, purl the purl stitch without letting it fall from the left needle.

3. Bring the thread to the back, knit the knit stitch, then let the two stitches fall.

On the next row, knit the stitches as now established.

BOBBLES

Bobbles, which form small balls, are often placed on a background of reverse stockinette stitch: they are frequently found with Irish stitches. They also accompany cable stitches and folklore motifs.

Bobbles are mostly made up of 4 stitches, but may vary in size and color, forming a contrast with the color of the background of the knitting.

THE 4-STITCH BOBBLE

1 and 2: This bobble is made in one stitch. Knit 4 stitches for the bobble as follows: knit 1, purl 1, knit 1 and purl 1 all in the same stitch. Turn the work and purl these 4 stitches. Turn the work over again and slide the first 2 stitches on the right needle, knit the next 2 stitches together and slip the 2 slipped stitches on these 2 stitches knitted together. One stitch remains.

NOTE

A small hole always forms under the bobble.

THE 5-STITCH BOBBLE

1. Form the 5-stitch knot stitch as follows: knit 1, purl 1, knit 1, purl 1, knit 1 all in the same stitch.

2 and 3. Turn the work and purl these 5 stitches. Turn the work over again and knit these 5 stitches, then turn again and purl the 5 stitches.

4 and 5. Turn again and slip the 4 stitches one by one over the fifth, beginning with the closest stitch. Finish the row.

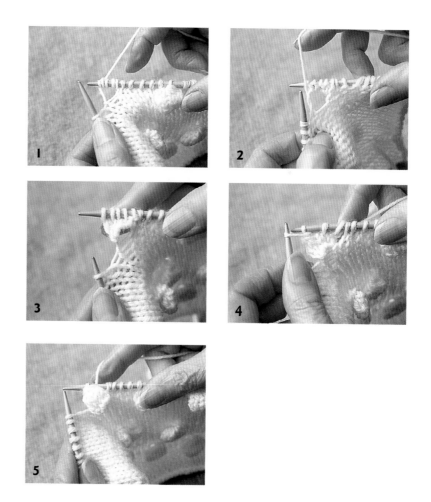

TWISTED STITCHES

Twisted stitches noticeably accentuate the raised quality of knit stitches placed on a background of reverse stockinette; they accentuate the structure of 1/1 rib stitch (see the photo opposite), and also form families of stitches accompanying panels of simple cable stitches or different fancy stitches found in Irish knitting.

TWISTED KNIT STITCH

NOTE

Moving diagonally, twisted stitches can form snake designs, zigzags or borders of cables. Playing with the twisted 1/1 rib stitch and the normal 1/1 rib stitch, you obtain a mosaic of raised stitches. Using twisted stitches makes a firm ribbing that doesn't stretch out of shape over time.

1 and 2. Place the right needle in the back thread of the stitch, knit the stitch. The base of the stitch will be twisted.

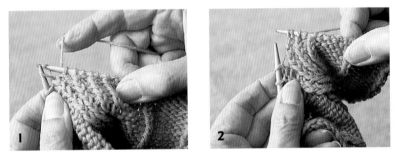

TWISTED PURL STITCH

1 and 2. Place the right needle in the back thread of the stitch, purl the stitch.

VARIATION

To make the twisted 1/1 ribs, on both right and wrong sides of work, knit the knit stitches as twisted ones and the purl stitches normally.

Men's Sailor Sweater

THE SWEATER

Size:
Large

Materials:
Bouton d'Or Superwash Croisière
(50 g/95 m) balls, 25 oz (700 g) in
the color of your choice
Pairs of size 3 (3-1/3 mm) and 6
(4-1/4 mm) needles
Cable needle

Stitches used:
2/2 rib stitch: K 2, P 2.
Fancy stitch (see grid)
Welt stitch over 6 rows

Gauge Swatch:
Working in fancy stitch on larger
needles, 22 sts and 34 rows = 4"
(10 cm).

NOTE

For a neater finish, place the neckband
stitches on a circular needle or a set of
4 needles: 37 on back, 17 on left front,
17 at center front, 17 on right front.
Knit in rounds of 2/2 ribbing for 1-1/2"
(4 cm). Bind off in ribbing.

INSTRUCTIONS

BACK
Cast on 118 stitches on smaller needles. Work 3" (8 cm) in 2/2 ribbing, increasing 17 sts evenly over last row, (135 sts).

With larger needles, follow the fancy stitch chart, on the next page, with 1 selvage st on each side.

At 25-1/4" (64 cm) in total length, work the pleat stitch pattern as follows: *K 1 row, P 1 row, K 2 rows, P 1 row, K 1 row*; repeat from * to * until 15 rows are completed. Bind off all the sts.

FRONT
Begin as you did for the back.

At 23-1/2" (60 cm) from beg, place the center 17 sts on a holder for neck. Work each side separately and at each neck edge, bind off 3 sts every other row once, 2 sts twice, 1 st once, (49 sts each side).

At 25-1/4" (64 cm) in total length, work 15 rows in pleat stitch as for back. Bind off all sts on each shoulder.

SLEEVES
Cast on 42 sts on smaller needles and work in 2/2 ribbing for 2-1/4" (6 cm), increasing 29 sts evenly over final row, (71 sts).

With larger needles, follow the fancy stitch chart, starting at A, and increase 1 st at each side every 8 rows 18 times. Work even on 107 sts to 19-1/4" (49 cm) in total length. Bind off all sts.

FINISHING TOUCHES

Weave the loose yarn ends into the work and lightly steam iron all the pieces on the back.

Sew the left shoulder. With smaller needles, pick up the 37 stitches on the back neck, then pick up the 18 on the left front edge, 17 sts from center front holder, and 18 sts on right front,

(90 sts). Work 1-1/2" (4 cm) in 2/2 ribbing. Bind off all stitches in ribbing. Seam right shoulder and neckband. Mark side edges of front and back 9-1/2" (24 cm) below shoulder seams. Attach sleeves between markers. Seam sleeves and sides of sweater.

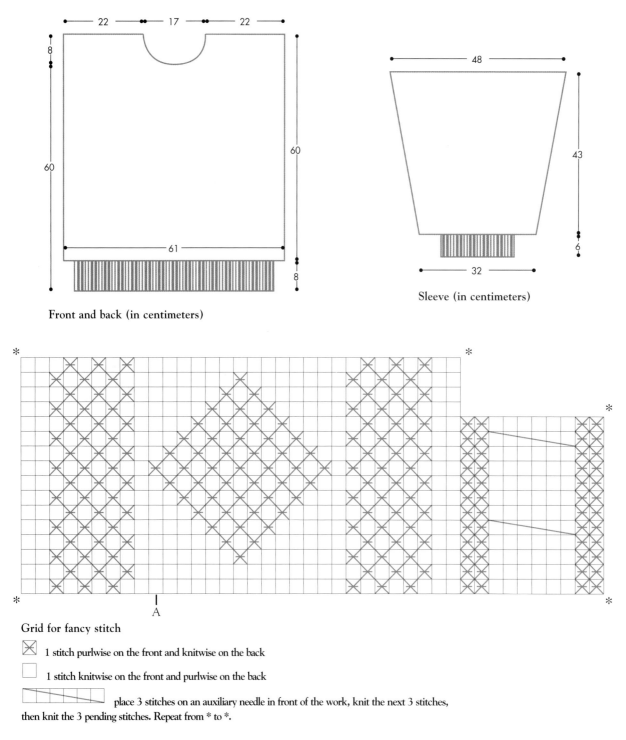

Front and back (in centimeters)

Sleeve (in centimeters)

Grid for fancy stitch

⊠ 1 stitch purlwise on the front and knitwise on the back

☐ 1 stitch knitwise on the front and purlwise on the back

▱ place 3 stitches on an auxiliary needle in front of the work, knit the next 3 stitches, then knit the 3 pending stitches. Repeat from * to *.

Dandy Wrist Muffs

THE WRIST MUFFS

Materials:

Bouton d'Or Dandy (50 g/80 m balls), 4 oz (100 g) in the color of your choice

Pair number 10 (6 mm) needles

Stitches used:

Reverse Stockinette stitch: P 1 row, K 1 row.

Tree of Life stitch (see pages 112–113)

INSTRUCTIONS

Cast on 32 stitches. Work 2-1/2" (6 cm) in reverse stockinette stitch. Now work as follows: Work 8 sts in reverse stockinette stitch, the center 16 sts in the Tree of Life motif, and 8 sts in reverse stockinette stitch.

Work as established until the Tree of Life motif has been worked 3 times, then work about 1" (2 cm) of reverse stockinette stitch. Bind off all stitches.

FINISHING TOUCHES

Cast on 32 stitches. Work 2-1/2" (6 cm) in reverse stockinette stitch. Now work as follows: Work 8 sts in reverse stockinette stitch, the center 16 sts in the Tree of Life motif, and 8 sts in reverse stockinette stitch.

Work as established until the Tree of Life motif has been worked 3 times, then work about 1" (2 cm) of reverse stockinette stitch. Bind off all stitches.

Multicolored Knitting

By using color, knitting can be enhanced by regular or irregular stripes and motifs of every kind to repeat or use singly: jacquard, Peruvian designs, intarsia, etc.

STRIPES

Stripes are formed by using several different-colored yarns. Changing the yarn must always occur at the beginning of the row, and the loose yarn ends are worked back into the knitting using a yarn needle. They can also be woven into the knitting. It is important to leave about 4" (10 cm) of yarn at each color change so that the ends may be easily worked in.

The color change forms neat rows on stockinette stitch, but takes on a completely different, irregular effect on reverse stockinette stitch at the first row worked in a new color.

WORKING THE YARN BACK IN

I to 3. Thread the hanging end of the yarn into a yarn needle (with a rounded tip). Pass the needle under about 2–3" (5–7 cm) worth of stitches on the back of the work, then cut the remainder of the yarn.

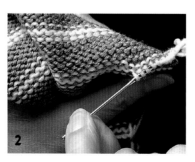

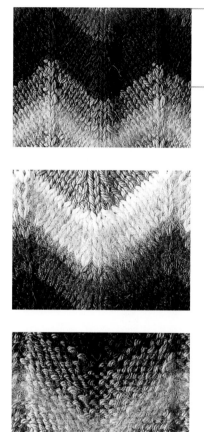

CLASSIC CHEVRONS IN STRIPES

This is a fantastic effect which allows you to use your leftover yarns in different colors and textures, and classic chevrons can be varied to your own wishes. While the materials may be diverse (mohair, angora, silk, laces, or wool), it is of utmost importance to use yarns of the same size and thickness.

Cast on stitches in a multiple of 16 plus 1.

Row 1: (Note: To increase, use make 1 between sts, or bar inc by working 2 sts in preceding st, or yo between sts for a lacy look.) *K 1 for rib st, K 2 tog, K 5 sts, inc 1, K 1 for rib st, inc 1, K 5 sts, dec 1 skp*; repeat from * to * across; end with a rib st.
Row 2: Purl all the stitches.
Repeat these two rows for pattern.

Change colors as desired, working as many rows of each color as you wish. The chevron design shows on the reverse side of work as well as on the front. The pointed top and bottom edges can be used for collars and sleeve edges or evened with rows of garter stitch.

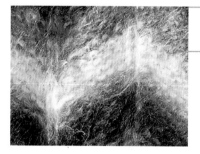

WAVY STITCHES

Wave stitches are an interesting variation of classic chevrons. In this case, the number of stitches must be in a multiple of 18, plus 1.

Row 1: K 1 st, inc 1 purlwise, P 6 sts, P 2 tog, K 1 st, P 2 tog, P 6 sts, inc 1 purlwise, K 1 st*; repeat from * to * across.
Row 2: P 1 purl st, *K 8 sts, P 1 st, K 8 sts, P 1 st*; repeat from * to * across.
Repeat these two rows.

JACQUARDS

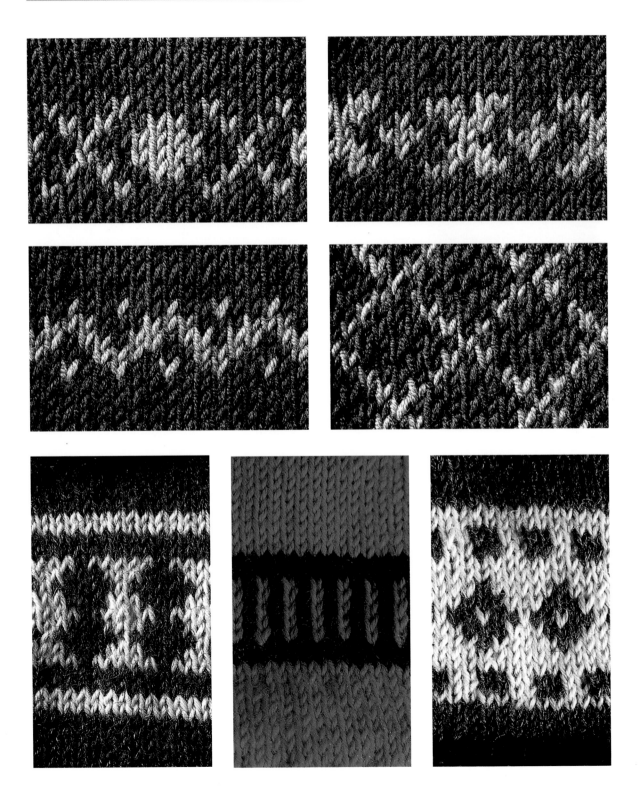

NOTE

Jacquard is knitted usually in stockinette stitch, the fingers of the right hand working the yarns. With a bit of practice, it is possible to use both hands, this sometimes called Norwegian knitting. The yarn on the index finger of the right hand is the foundation color while the yarn on the index finger of the left hand carries the second color.

Jacquard knitting is characterized by a composition of several motifs, with at least two colors per row. We owe the name of this style of knitting to Joseph-Marie Jacquard (1752–1834) who invented, at the dawn of the industrial age, jacquard knitting which permitted for the first time the simultaneous weaving of different designs using different colors. This system, which revolutionized traditional weaving techniques, was then adapted to knitting machines, integrating them into a system of perforated cards which made them perform better and allowed the use of more than one color.

Following jacquard models, the designs either partially or completely decorate the knitted piece. Small, usually geometric motifs, are usually connected with Fair Isle knitting (the name of the islands situated to the north of Great Britain); they are made with the yarns of the local area, which suggest their origin by the subdued colors that call to mind the particular environment of these islands. Peruvian motifs, reproduced on the Andean hats and ponchos popular during the hippie movement, are also part of the jacquard family.

The motifs used to make jacquard patterns are often designed on a piece of graph paper with each square representing a stitch and each line a row. Different symbols are used to represent different colors and motifs. Following these graphs shows the progression of the motifs. You will find a blank graph on page 209 to use for your own motifs.

Manually, there are several methods which allow you to work jacquards. The changing of colors is done across the back, along the row. The motifs are traditionally knitted in stockinette stitch. You cross the yarns at each color change to prevent holes in the work.

Two methods are used for making jacquards. They are based on the size of the motifs, and are called simple jacquard and double jacquard.

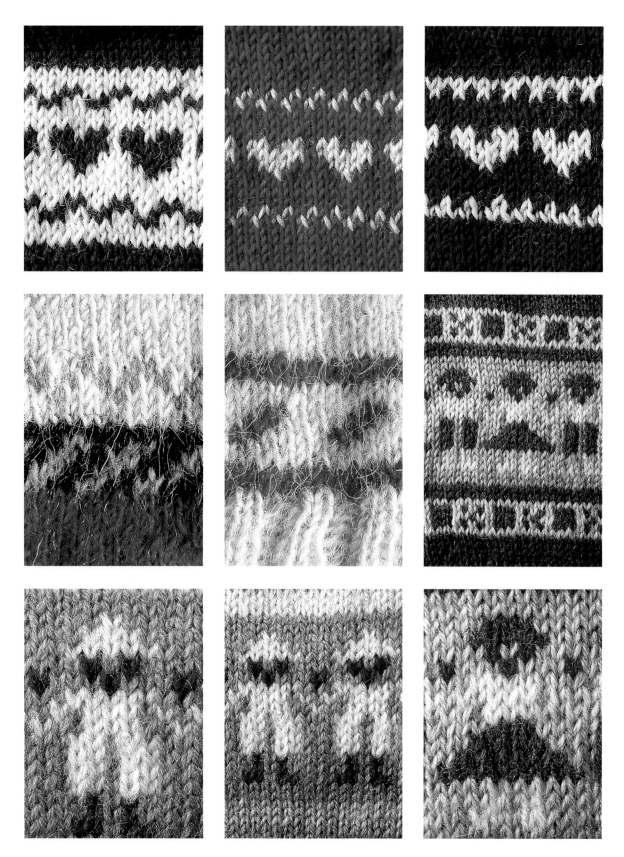

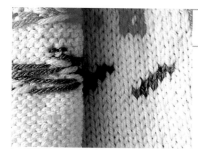

SINGLE JACQUARD

For small motifs no more than 5 stitches, the yarn is worked forward and crosses on the back of the work, floating at each color change. This is what we call single jacquard. The pattern is formed on the front with the various colored yarns carried on the back.

1 to 3. Knit the motifs following the graph for the placement of colors in the row.

4 and 5. On the back of the work, hold the second color yarn in your left hand while knitting the stitches with the other color.

NOTE

It is important to maintain an even tension throughout your knitting. If it is too tight, your yarns will bunch up, looking uneven and narrowing the width of the piece. If the tension is too loose, there will be spaces between the color changes.

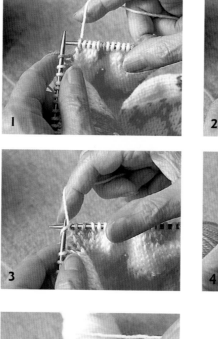

NOTE

The different yarns used are never knotted together at their ends, but worked into the knitting with the help of a yarn needle, either into the selvage or on the back of a row. A gentle steaming will even out slight irregularities.

WOVEN JACQUARD

Woven jacquard, needs to be used when the yarn has to be carried over more than 5 stitches. The different yarns are "woven" on the back. They cross in a permanent manner, one stitch over two, thus giving a double thickness to the knitting. This work tightens your pattern and prevents long, annoying floating threads on the back. On the back, place your needle in the stitch then pass the unused yarn under the yarn which will be knitted and over the right needle.

1 and 2. Finish knitting the stitch, without passing the second thread, then knit the next stitch normally. The yarns will then cross every two stitches.

3. On the purl rows, pass the pending colored thread in front of the one which will be knitted, then between the two points of the needles.

4. Then knit the stitch on the back, keeping the working thread in front of the work.

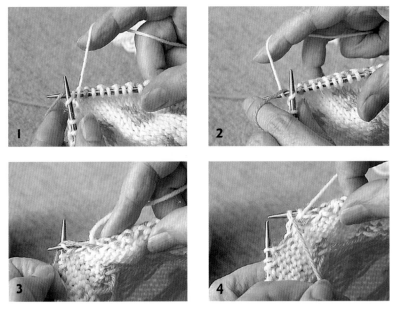

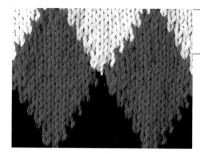

INTARSIA

As with jacquard, intarsias, also called "isolated motifs," are drawn on graphs serving as patterns for their creation.

You must, again, as with jacquard, cross the threads on the back of the knitting to prevent holes when you change colors. It is practical to prepare the small skeins of the colors being used to work more easily. Bobbins (pegs) provided for this use are available in craft shops; you can, if you prefer, use pieces of cardboard around which you wind different yarns.

DO NOT TANGLE THE THREADS

1 to 5. Place the skeins next to each other in the order defined by the pattern you are making. Then knit them by crossing the threads, holding the old color to the left as you bring the new color up from under the old to work the next stitch. Drop the old color. At end of row, check that each yarn is untangled and hanging straight down.

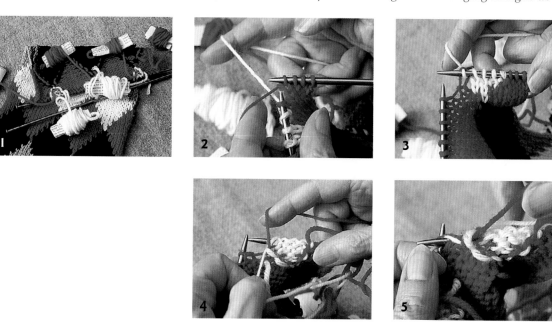

INTERLACING

This technique designates a procedure that is part of colored knitting because it forms a sort of patchwork. The knitting here is made up of different colored rectangles, knitted individually then joined in the course of the work. Interlacing, most often made in different colors, can also be made in a single color and decorated by fancy stitches.

Techniques and basic principles

Interlacing requires a base of triangles linked together and forming a horizontal border. The number of stitches used for each of these triangles thus determines the size of the interlacing rectangles.

It is important to make a fairly large sampler; it will serve as a base for your calculations for the knitting to be made, whether it is a pillow cover, a lap blanket, or a cardigan. The interlacing stitch has a tendency to curl at the edges, so an ironing of the sampler is needed before beginning to make the real model.

In the case of a pull-over, you should look for a squared pattern as the interlacing does not allow for rounded edges.

The Sampler

For a sampler, cast on 40 stitches and begin with a row of triangles.

First Triangle

Rows 1 and 2: K 2 sts (leave the stitches pending on the needle), turn; P 2 sts, turn.

Rows 3 and 4: K 3 sts, turn; P 3 sts, turn.

Rows 5 and 6: K 4 sts, P 4 sts.

Rows 7 and 8: K 5 sts, P 5 sts.

Rows 9 and 10: K 6 sts, P 6 sts.

Rows 11 and 12: K 7 sts, P 7 sts.

Rows 13 and 14: K 8 sts, P 8 sts.

Rows 15 and 16: K 9 sts, P 9 sts.

Row 17: K 10 sts; leave the stitches pending on the right needle.

Form the next three triangles as you did the first, each time keeping the stitches pending. Then knit the first row of rectangles with a triangle at each side as follows:

Triangle on the left edge

Rows 1 and 2: P2 sts, turn, slip 1 st, K 1 st, turn.

Rows 3 and 4: P 2 sts in the first st by purling in the back strand and then purling in the front strand (= 1 increase), P 2 tog, turn, slip 1 st, K 2 sts, turn.

Rows 5 and 6: P 2 sts in the first st, P 1 st, P 2 tog, turn, slip 1 st, K 3 sts. Turn after each row.

Rows 7 and 8: P 2 sts in the first st, P 2 sts, P 2 tog, turn, slip 1 st, K 4 sts.

Rows 9 and 10: P 2 sts in the first st, P 3 sts, P 2 tog, turn, slip 1 st, K 5 sts.

Rows 11 and 12: P 2 sts in the first st, P 4 sts, P 2 tog, turn, slip 1 st, K 6 sts.

Rows 13 and 14: P 2 sts in the first st, P 5 sts, P 2 tog, turn, slip 1 st, K 7 sts.

Rows 15 and 16: P 2 sts in the first st, P 6 sts, P 2 tog, turn, slip 1 st, K 8 sts.

Row 17: P 2 sts in the first st, P 7 sts, P 2 tog. Leave the 10 sts pending on the needle.

First Rectangle

Working on the wrong side, use right needle to pick up the 10 stitches on the right needle of the edge of the fourth base triangle, inserting the needle from back to front of the work and knitting them purlwise; turn.

Rows 1 and 2: Slip 1 st, K 9 sts, turn, P 9 sts, P 2 tog (the last of the 10 plus 1 st of the next triangle), turn.

Repeat these two rows nine more times (up to the end of the triangle's sts), then leave these 10 sts pending on the right needle.

Form the next two rectangles in the same manner, picking up the stitches on the third then on the second base triangle.

Triangle on the right edge

Pick up (as you did for the rectangles) 10 sts on the second side of the first base triangle; turn.

Rows 1 and 2: K 10 sts, turn, P 8 sts, P 2 tog, turning after each row throughout.

Rows 3 and 4: K 9 sts, turn, P 7 sts, P 2 purl tog.

Rows 5 and 6: K 8 sts, turn, P 6 sts, P 2 tog.

Rows 7 and 8: K 7 sts, turn, P 5 sts, P 2 tog.

Rows 9 and 10: K 6 sts, turn, P 4 sts, P 2 tog.

Rows 11 and 12: K 5 sts, turn, P 3 sts, P 2 tog.

Rows 13 and 14: K 4 sts, turn, P 2 sts, P 2 tog.

Rows 15 and 16: K 3 sts, turn, P 1 st, P 2 tog.

Rows 17 and 18: K 2 sts, turn, P 2 tog, leave the remaining stitch pending.

Continue working the second row of rectangles.

First Rectangle

With the right needle, pick up 9 sts on the back of the interior border of the triangle; turn.

Rows 1 and 2: Slip 1 st, P 9 sts, turn, K 9 sts, dec 1 skp taking up 1 st of the rectangle of the first row, turn.

Repeat these two rows 9 times, then leave the 10 sts pending on the right needle.

Form the three other rectangles in the same way, picking up the sts on the edges of the next rectangles. Repeat these rows of rectangles until you obtain the desired height.

To finish the work, there are two options, which depend on the number of rows of rectangles.

. . . If the number of rows of rectangles is even:

The wrong side of the work faces you. The final row is made up of large triangles with a small triangle at each side.

Small left triangle

Rows 1 and 2: P 2 tog, turn, K 1 st, 1 increase, turn.

Rows 3 and 4: Slip 1 st, P 2 tog, turn, K 2 sts, 1 increase, turn.

Rows 5 and 6: Slip 1 stitch, P 1 st, P 2 tog, turn, K 3 sts, 1 increase.

Rows 7 and 8: Slip 1 stitch, P 2 sts, P 2 tog, turn, K 4 sts, 1 increase.

Rows 9 and 10: Slip 1 stitch, P 3 sts, P 2 tog, turn, K 5 sts, 1 increase.

Rows 11 and 12: P 2 tog, P 3 sts, P 2 tog, turn, K 5 sts.

Rows 13 and 14: P 2 tog, P 2 sts, P 2 tog, turn, K 4 sts.

Rows 15 and 16: P 2 tog, P 1 st, P 2 tog, turn, K 3 sts.

Row 17: P 2 tog, then bind off the second stitch on the first and leave the remaining stitch pending on the needle.

Large triangles

Pick up the 9 sts on the edge of the rectangle by inserting the needle from the back to the front of the work.

Rows 1 and 2: K 10 sts, turn, P 2 tog, P 7 sts, P 2 tog taking up the one st of the next rectangle.

Rows 3 and 4: K 9 sts, turn, P 2 tog, P 6 sts, P 2 tog.

Rows 5 and 6: K 8 sts, turn, P 2 tog, P 5 sts, P 2 tog.

Rows 7 and 8: K 7 sts, turn, P 2 tog, P 4 sts, P 2 tog.

Rows 9 and 10: K 6 sts, turn, P 2 tog, P 3 sts, P 2 tog.

Rows 11 and 12: K 5 sts, turn, P 2 tog, P 2 sts, P 2 tog.

Rows 13 and 14: K 4 sts, turn, P 2 tog, P 1 st, P 2 tog.

Rows 15 and 16: K 3 sts, turn, P 2 tog twice.

Rows 17 and 18: K 2 sts, turn, P 1 st, P 2 tog.

Rows 19 and 20: K 2 sts, turn, slip 1 st, P 2 tog, bind off the slipped stitch on the stitch obtained and leave the remaining stitch pending on the needle. Knit the next two triangles in the same manner.

Small right triangle

Pick up the 9 stitches from the edge of the last rectangle.

Rows 1 and 2: K 10 sts, turn, P 2 tog, P 6 sts, P 2 tog.

Rows 3 and 4: K 8 sts, turn, P 2 tog, P 4 sts, P 2 tog.

Rows 5 and 6: K 6 knit stitches, turn, P 2 tog, P 2 sts, P 2 tog.

Rows 7 and 8: K 4 sts, turn, P 2 tog twice.

Rows 9 and 10: K 2 sts, turn, P 2 tog.

Cut the thread and slip it into the pending stitch.

. . . If the number of rows of triangles is uneven:

The right side of the work faces you. The last row is made up only of large triangles.

First triangle

Pick up 9 stitches from the edge of the triangle.

Rows 1 and 2: Slip 1 st, P 9 sts, turn, K 9 sts, dec 1 skp by knitting 1 st of the rectangle.

Rows 3 and 4: Slip 1 st, P 7 sts, P 2 tog, turn, K 8 sts, dec 1 skp.

Rows 5 and 6: Slip 1 st, P 6 sts, P 2 tog, turn, K 7 sts, dec 1 skp.

Rows 7 and 8: Slip 1 st, P 5 sts, P 2 tog, turn, K 6 sts, dec 1 skp.

Rows 9 and 10: Slip 1 st, P 4 sts, P 2 tog, turn, K 5 sts, dec 1 skp.

Rows 11 and 12: Slip 1 st, P 3 sts, P 2 tog, turn, K 4 sts, dec 1 skp.

Rows 13 and 14: Slip 1 st, P 2 sts, P 2 tog, turn, K 3 sts, dec 1 skp.

Rows 15 and 16: Slip 1 st, P 1 st, P 2 tog, turn, K 2 sts, dec 1 skp.

Rows 17 and 18: Slip 1 st, P 2 tog, turn, K 1 st, dec 1 skp.

Rows 19 and 20: P 2 tog, turn, dec 1 skp, leaving the remaining st pending on the right needle.

Work the next triangles in the same manner, then fasten off the final stitch of the row.

Jacquard Knee-Socks and Scarf

THE KNEE-SOCKS

Sizes:

Age 2–4 years

Materials:

Anny Blatt Baby Blatt (50g/180m balls) 1-3/4 oz (50 g) in the colors of your choice

5 double-pointed needles number 0 (2 cm)

3/8" (1 cm) wide elastic

Stitches used:

Stockinette stitch (knitted around): All rounds knitted.

Small motif jacquard (see grid)

Cat's tooth stitch

Gauge Swatch:

In stockinette st on larger needles 29 sts and 37 rounds = 4" (10 cm).

INSTRUCTIONS

THE KNEE-SOCKS, shown at the right of the phtograph

Begin with the top of the leg.

With large dpns and main color, cast on 48 stitches. Work 8 rnds in stockinette st. Work 1 rnd of cat's tooth: *Yo, K 2 tog*; repeat from * to * across. Work 12 rnds in St st. Attach contrast color and work 16 rnds of jacquard grid (page 142). Cut contrast color; continue in St st with main color only for 4 rnds.

On next rnd, begin decreases for the calves: Dec 1 with skp, K 1 (center back st), K 2 tog, then complete rnd. Repeat dec rnd every 10 rows twice more, (42 sts).

At 8-1/4" (21 cm) in total length, cut yarn. Begin heel using just 2 needles: On one needle, place the center back st and the 10 sts from each side, maintaining their original order. Work these 21 sts back and forth as follows: On RS rows, work K 1, then repeat (slip 1 st, K 1) across; on WS rows, purl all sts. Repeat these 2 rows for 1-3/4" (4.5 cm), ending with a purl row.

To finish heel: K 13, skp, turn; P 6, P 2 tog, turn; K 7, skp, turn; P 8 sts, P 2 tog, turn. Continue in this manner until you have used up all the pending sts.

Now begin work again on the set of 5 double-pointed needles. Place a marker on needle for beg of round. On next round, K 13 sts, then pick up 10 sts along edge of heel, K across 21 pending for top of foot, pick up 10 sts along opposite edge of heel, (54 sts). Knit all sts and decrease 1 st at each side of foot, taking 1 st from the edge of heel and 1 st from the top to form each decrease. Continue in St st and repeat decreases every 4 rnds 5 times more, (42 sts rem). Knit even for 2-3/4" (7 cm). Form the toe of the sock by decreasing as follows: K 15 sts, K 2 tog, K 1 st (side st), skp, K 15 sts, K 2 tog, K 1 st (side st), skp, K 2 sts.

Continue decreasing 1 st before and after each side st every other rnd 4 more times (there will be 2 fewer sts between the side sts after each decrease rnd, 22 sts rem). Sew toe closed with grafting stitch

THE SCARF

Materials

Bouton d'Or Croisière (50g/95m balls), 1-3/4 oz (50 g) in the color of your choice
1 pair size 6 (4-1/4 mm) needles
Cable needle

Stitches used

Seed stitch: *K 1, P 1*; work in the opposite order each row.
Cable stitch: work over 6 stitches and 8 rows.

Gauge Swatch:

In seed st 24 sts and 26 rows = 4" (10 cm).

(see page 195) to avoid an uncomfortable seam at the toes. As you graft the stitches together, match stitch for stitch at top and bottom. Fold down and sew in place the top hem, slipping the elastic inside. Turn the socks inside out and lightly steam them with an iron.

THE SCARF

Cast on 30 stitches. Work 6 rows of seed stitch. Establish pattern on next row: Work *6 sts in seed st, 6 sts in Stockinette st for cable*; repeat from * to * once; end 6 sts in seed st.

Work as established and on fifth row turn cables: For first cable, cross the stitches to the right by slipping 3 sts to a cable needle and holding it behind work, K next 3 sts on left needle, then K the 3 sts from the cable needle. For the second cable, cross the stitches to the left, holding the 3 sts on the cable needle in front of work. Work 3 more rows as established, then repeat these 8 rows.

At 36" (92 cm) in total length, work 6 rows in seed stitch. Bind off all sts in pattern.

Work the loose yarn ends into the knitting and lightly steam iron the piece on the back, making sure not to crush the cables.

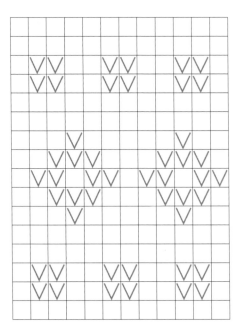

Jacquard grid

Child's Little Doggy Sweater

THE SWEATER

Size:
4–5 years

Materials:
Anny Blatt Number 5 (50 g/95 m balls)
10-1/2 oz (300 g) off white
1-3/4 oz (50 g) each palm green and black
Pair each size 3 (3-1/4 mm) and 6 (4-1/4 cm) needles

Stitches used:
1/1 rib stitch: K 1, P 1.
Stockinette stitch: K 1 row, P 1 row.
Stockinette jacquard (see grids)

Gauge Swatch:
In stockinette stitch on larger needles, 22 sts and 30 rows = 4" (10 cm).

INSTRUCTIONS

BACK
With smaller needles and the off-white yarn, cast on 90 sts. Work 1-1/2" (4 cm) in 1/1 rib stitch.

With larger needles, work 4 rows in stockinette stitch. Attaching and discontinuing colors as needed, continue in St st and follow jacquard grid 2 for 6 rows: Begin at right and repeat across, ending center rows with a block. Then work grid 1 for 13 rows: Work 7 sts; on center 76 sts, follow grid with M at center, work 7 sts. Then continue with off-white only.

At 16" (41 cm) in total length, bind off 9 sts at beg of next 6 rows for shoulders. Bind off remaining 36 sts at center for neck edge.

FRONT
Begin as you did for the back.

At 14" (36 cm) from beg, bind off center 12 sts for front neck. Work each side separately and at each neck edge, bind off every other row 3 sts once, 2 sts twice, then dec 1 st 3 times, (27 sts each side).

At 16" (41 cm) in total length, at each shoulder edge, bind off 9 sts every other row 3 times.

SLEEVES
Cast on 43 sts on smaller needle. Work 1-1/2" (4 cm) in 1/1 rib stitch.

With larger needles, work in stockinette stitch, increasing 5 sts evenly over first row, then increase 1 st each side every 6 rows 12 times, (72 sts).

At 10-1/2" (27 cm) in total length, bind off 12 sts at beg of next 4 rows, then bind off remaining 24 sts.

FANCY COLLAR

Cast 96 stitches on a circular number 3 needle (or on a set of four 2-pointed needles) and knit 2.5 cm in 1/1 rib stitch, then attach this border to the collar with backstitches in the stitches of the edge and the sweater.

FINISHING TOUCHES

Lightly steam-iron all the pieces on the back to even out the expected irregularities at the color changes.

Sew the left shoulder. With smaller needles, pickup and K 35 stitches along the back neck edge, then 25 sts on left front neck edge, 11 sts at center front, 25 on front neck edge, (96 sts). Work 1" (2.5 cm) in 1/1 rib stitch. Bind off in ribbing.

Sew the second shoulder and the edge of the collar.

Attach the sleeves and sew them closed, along with the sides of the sweater.

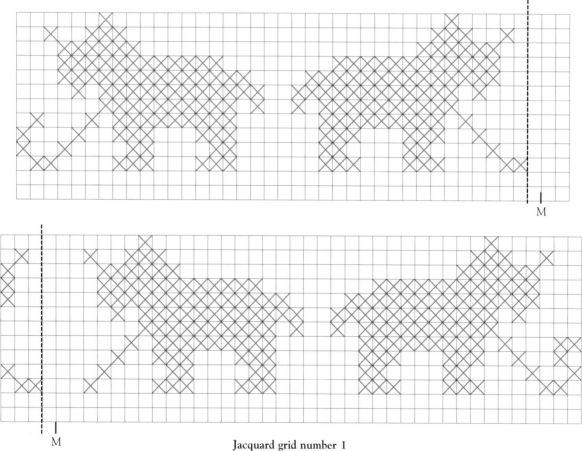

Jacquard grid number 1

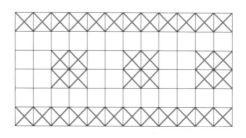

Jacquard grid number 2

Openwork Knitting

Openwork knitting, as the name indicates, presents beautiful open designs formed by stitches classified among the lace stitches. They can be made independently or accompanied by other families of stitches.

The chosen motifs are often geometrical or evoke nature. They are made up of leafy patterns, ferns, lacy diamonds, open chevrons, feathers, and fans. All these lacy patterns contribute to the lightness of the knitting, and the types of yarns used for these stitches, such as kid mohair, make it even lighter. Mercerized cottons allow you to maximize the lightweight quality of summer sweaters.

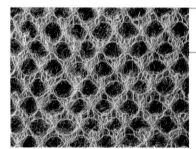

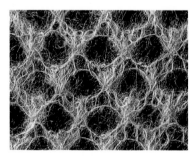

CAT'S EYE STITCH

The number of stitches must be a multiple of 4, plus 2 selvage stitches for the sampler.

Row 1: 1 selvage stitch, *yo, P 4 tog*, 1 selvage stitch.
Row 2: 1 selvage stitch, * K 1 st, then K 1, P 1 and K 1 all in the loop formed by the yo on the preceding row*; repeat from * to *; end 1 selvage stitch.
Row 3: knit.
Repeat these three rows.

NOTE

Very simple openwork stitches can for example be used for "trendy" fashion accessories, and are very pretty if made in kid mohair. Irish knits, for example, are often lightened by using the combination of cable knits and lace stitches.

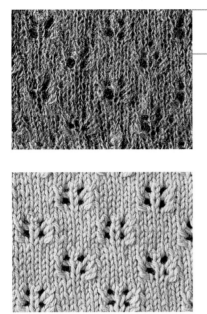

BUTTERFLY STITCH

The number of stitches must be a multiple of 10, plus 2 selvages for the sampler.

Row 1: 1 selvage stitch, *K 2 tog, yo, K 1, yo, skp, K 5*; repeat from * to *; end 1 selvage stitch.

Row 2 and all even rows: Purl all stitches, including yo.

Row 3: Repeat row 1.

Row 5: Knit all stitches.

Row 7: 1 selvage stitch, *K 5, K 2 tog, yo, K 1, yo, skp*; repeat from * to *; end 1 selvage stitch.

Row 9: Repeat row 7.

Row 11: Knit all stitches.

Row 12: Repeat row 2.

Repeat these 12 rows for pattern.

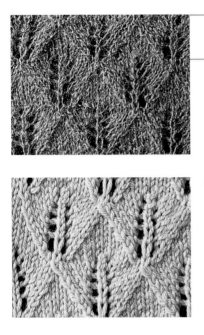

FERN STITCH (1)

There are many fern stitches, both simple and complex. The following explanation for this stitch is of English origin.

The number of stitches must be in a multiple of 12, plus 3 stitches, 2 of which are selvages, for the sampler.

Row 1: 1 selvage st, *K 4 sts, K 2 tog, yo, K 1 st, yo, SKP, K 3 sts*; repeat from * to *; end K 1 st, 1 selvage st.

Row 2 and all even rows: 1 selvage st, P 13 sts, 1 selvage st.

Row 3: 1 selvage st, *K 3 sts, K 2 tog, K 1 st, yo, K 1 st, yo, K 1 st, SKP, K 2 sts*; repeat from * to *; end K 1 st, 1 selvage st.

Row 5: 1 selvage st, *K 2 sts, K 2 tog, K 2 sts, yo, K 1 st, yo, K 2 sts, SKP, K1 st*; repeat from * to *; end K 1 st, 1 selvage st.

Row 7: 1 selvage st, * K 1 st, K 2 tog, K 3 sts, yo, K 1 st, yo, K 3 sts, SKP*; repeat from * to *; end K 1 st, 1 selvage st.

Row 9: 1 selvage st, K 2 tog, *K 4 sts, yo, K 1 st, yo, K 4 sts, 1 double knit decrease (see page 42)*; repeat from * to *; 1 selvage st. At the end of the row, replace the double slipped stitch with SKP.

Row 11: 1 selvage st, * K 1 st, yo, SKP, K 7 sts, K 2 tog, yo*; repeat from * to *; end K 1 st, 1 selvage st.

Row 13: 1 selvage st, *K 1 st, yo, K 1 st, SKP, K 5 sts, K 2 tog, K 1 st, yo*; repeat from * to *; end K 1 st, 1 selvage st.

Row 15: 1 selvage st, *K 1 st, yo, K 2 sts, SKP, K 3 sts, K 2 tog, K 2 sts, yo*; repeat from * to *; end K 1 st, 1 selvage st.

Row 17: 1 selvage st, *K 1 st, yo, K 3 sts, SKP, K 1 st, K 2 tog, K 3 sts, yo*; repeat from * to * ; end K 1 st, 1 selvage st.

Row 19: 1 selvage st, *K 1 st, yo, K 4 sts, 1 double decrease, K 4 sts, yo*; repeat from * to *; end K 1 st, 1 selvage st.

Row 20: Repeat row 2.

Repeat these twenty rows for pattern.

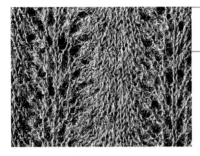

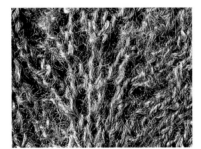

FERN STITCH (2)

The number of stitches must be in a multiple of 17, plus 2 selvage stitches.

Row 1: 1 selvage st, *(K 2 tog) 3 times, (yo, K 1) 5 times, yo, SKP 3 times*; repeat from * to *; end 1 selvage st.
Row 2: Purl the stitches, including yo.
Row 3: Knit.
Row 4: Purl
Repeat these four rows for pattern.

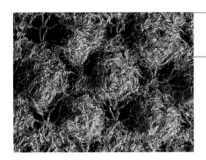

MADEIRA STITCH

The number of stitches must be in a multiple of 12, plus 5.

Rows 1 through 6: K 2 sts, *K 1 st, yo, K 4 sts, P 3 tog, K 4 sts, yo*; repeat from * to *; end the row with K 3 sts.
Rows 7 through 12: K 2 sts, P 2 tog, *K 4 sts, yo, K 1 st, yo, K 4 sts, P 3 tog*; repeat from * to *; end the row with P 2 tog (instead of 3) and K 2 sts.
Repeat these twelve rows.

Airy Baby Blankets and Stole in Kid Mohair

THE BLANKETS

Dimensions:
11-1/2" x 39-1/2" (28 x 100 cm)

Materials:
Anny Blatt Fine Kid (50 g/225 m ball) 1-3/4 oz (50 g) in Colocynth 092
Anny Blatt Fine Kid (50 g/225 m ball) 1-3/4 oz (50 g) in Platinum 443 or Callisto 086
Pair size 10 (6 mm) needles

Stitches used:
Cat's eye stitch

Gauge Swatch:
20 sts and 30 rows = 4" (10 cm)

THE STOLE

Dimensions:
20" x 63" (50 x 160 cm)

Materials:
Anny Blatt Fine Kid (50 g/225 m ball) 1-3/4 oz (50 g) in Ecru 182
Pair size 4 (3.5 mm) needles

Stitches used:
1/1 rib stitch: K 1, P 1.
Stockinette stitch: K 1 row, P 1 row.

Gauge Swatch:
Working in stockinette stitch, 24 sts and 34 rows = 4" (10 cm).

INSTRUCTIONS

THE BLANKETS
Cast on 58 stitches. Work the cat's eye stitch as follows:

Row 1: 1 selvage stitch, *yo, P 4 tog*, repeat from * to *; end 1 selvage stitch.
Row 2: 1 selvage stitch, *K 1 st, then work K 1 st, P 1 st and K 1 st all in the loop of the yo on the preceding row*; repeat from * to *; end 1 selvage stitch.
Row 3: Knit.
Repeat these three rows for pattern.

At 39-1/2" (100 cm) in total length, ending with a row 2, smoothly bind off all the stitches.

THE STOLE
Cast on 120 stitches. Work 1-1/4" (3 cm) in 1/1 ribbing. Continuing to work 6 stitches and beginning and end of rows in 1/1 ribbing, work center 108 stitches in stockinette stitch. At 61-3/4" (157 cm) in total length, work 1-1/4" (3 cm) in 1/1 ribbing. Bind off all stitches in ribbing.

[This works for stole as shown]
Cast on 120 stitches. Working 1 st at each end as a selvage stitch work remaining stitches in stockinette stitch for 1-1/4" (3 cm). Purl 1 row on right side. Then starting with a purl row, continue in stockinette stitch.

At 63" (160 cm), purl 1 row on right side. Then starting with a purl row, continue in stockinette stitch for 1-1/4" (3 cm) more. Bind off all sts.

Fold hems to wrong side along purl row and sew in place.

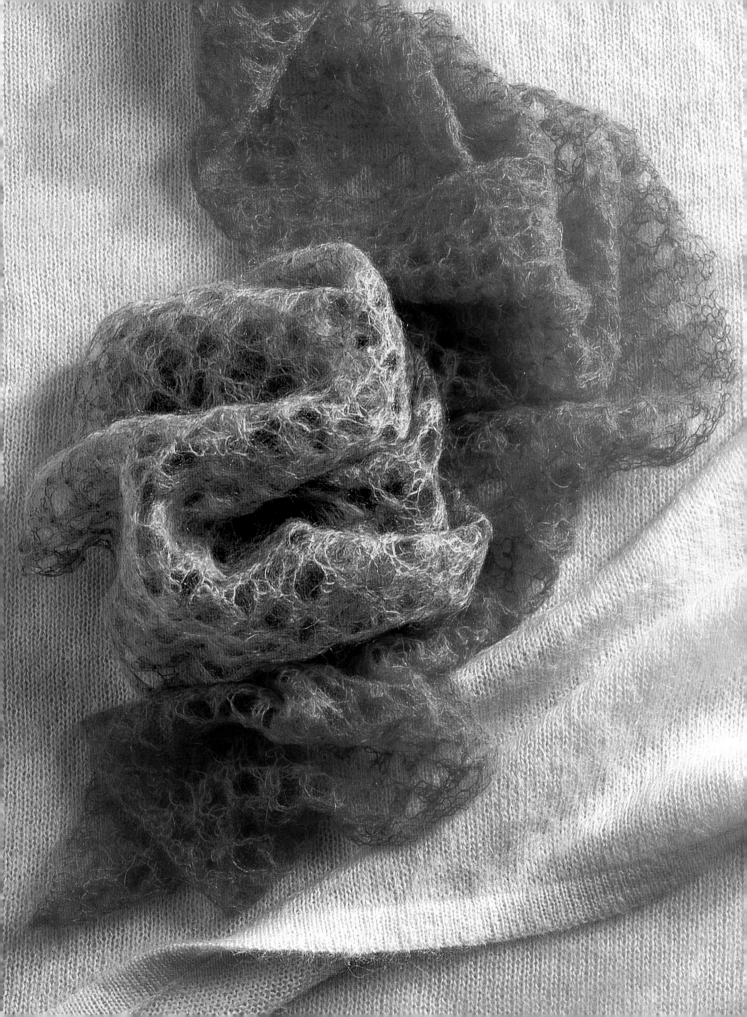

Fashion Collar in Kid Mohair

COLLAR

Dimensions
12-1/2" x 55" (32 x 140 cm)

Materials
Anny Blatt Fine Kid Mohair
(50g/225m balls) 3-1/2 oz (100 g)
in the color of your choice
Pair size 10 (6 mm) needles

Stitches used
Madeira stitch

Gauge Swatch:
In Madeira stitch, 20 sts and 32
rows = 4" (10 cm).

INSTRUCTIONS

Cast 65 stitches. Work in Madeira stitch as follows:

Rows 1 through 6: K 2 sts, *K 1 st, yo, K 4 sts, P 3 tog, K 4 sts, yo*; repeat from * to *; end with K 3 sts.

Rows 7 through 12: K 2 sts, P 2 tog, *K 4 sts, yo, K 1 st, yo, K 4 sts, P 3 tog*; repeat from * to *; end row with P 2 tog (instead of 3) and K 2 sts. Repeat these twelve rows.

At 55" (140 cm) in total length, bind off all the stitches.

4

Shapes and Finishing Touches

You must carefully plan the placement of buttonholes before making them, whether they are situated on a separate border, an integrated border, or on a border of picked-up stitches. To make the calculation for the placement easier, in the latter case, you can knit the button border (which will hold the button first); this will serve as a guide for the positioning of the buttonholes.

You must also take into account the size of the buttons: a domed button requires more space to pass through the buttonhole than a flat button. Finally, remember that buttonholes will expand with use, so slightly reduce their size in relation to the buttons.

LAYETTE BUTTONHOLE

This is the easiest to make: on the front of the knitting, make a yarn over and then knit two stitches together; on the opposite side, knit the stitch as it appears, and then the yarn over knitwise or purlwise in keeping with the stitch you are using.

1 and 2. The layette buttonhole forms a small eyelet through which you can also thread a cord or ribbon if the pattern requires.

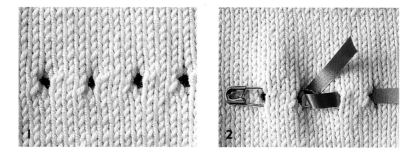

THE HORIZONTAL BUTTONHOLE

For the horizontal buttonhole, bind off, based on the size of the button, a few stitches on the right side of the knitting. In the following row, cast on the same number of stitches with a simple casting on and continue the row.

It is very wise to stagger the placement of the buttonholes one stitch in relation to the center of the band on which the buttons are sewn to counteract the tension exerted by the buttons: to the left if it is a woman's garment, and to the right if it is a man's garment.

THE VERTICAL BUTTONHOLE

For the vertical buttonhole, you must divide the knitting in two at the place of the buttonhole, knit each part separately up to the desired height and then reunite the two parts, respecting the direction of the knitting.

ADVICE

Buttonholes can also then be embroidered, as in sewing. Use a silk thread in a matching shade to reinforce the eyelets and to prevent rapid wear on the garment.

4. Borders

Borders may be integrated into the knitting; they can be picked up or added on, and they signal the end of the knitting. Made carefully, they are a mark of class and distinction.

INTEGRATED BORDERS

HORIZONTAL BORDERS

These are the ones which begin a work. They are knitted in a fancy stitch, different from the one used for the rest of the work. They are frequently done in rib stitches, but also in garter stitch (1) or seed stitch (2), to prevent the knitting from rolling.

VERTICAL BORDERS

The stitches necessary for the border are cast on at the beginning of the work to be knitted at the same time as the rest of the knitting. They are often in 1/1 rib stitch, but can also be done in garter stitch (1) or seed stitch (2) to differentiate them from the rest of the work. It is of course important to remember from the beginning to form the buttonholes.

PICKED UP BORDERS

The stitches are picked up with a needle, often a bit thinner than those used for the rest of the knitting, between the first two stitches of the edge. The shoulders are sewn and stitches are picked up along the neck edge for the neckband or collar.

1 and 2. The stitches are counted and picked up in such a way as to obtain a border which will neither shrink nor stretch the work. When done in the garter stitch, seed stitch, or stockinette stitch, usually three stitches are picked up every four rows.

For a ribbed border on edges, knit a sampler and place it on the edge of the work, easing it slightly. Count the number of stitches needed, then distribute the buttonholes, if needed. At the end of the work, smoothly bind off all the stitches as they present themselves.

For a sleeveless garment, you may want to tighten the final row on each side of the sewn shoulder and the sides, forming a few decreases. In this instance, the border will take on the shape of the arms better.

ADDED BORDERS

For a vertical border, cast the required number of stitches on a needle (a smaller sized one than you used for the rest of the knitting), respecting the symmetry of the stitch.

1 and 2. When the length of the border is achieved, leave the stitches pending to integrate them in the edge of the round neckband, for example, or bind them off smoothly. Sew this border onto the edge using a stitch-to-stitch method (see page 194).

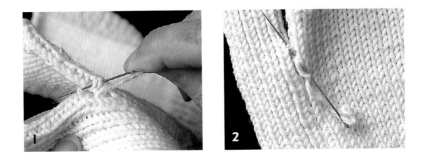

The shape of the neck trim is defined by the pattern. The most classic neckbands are round or crew neck and v-neck bands, along with their many variations, from the most traditional to the most fancy, based on the influences of fashion.

To finish a neckband requires special attention because once it is finished, it must be very flexible to allow the head to pass through it without gaping or warping.

ROUND COLLARS

It can be finished simply with a self band or with a ribbed band, with a turtleneck or fold-down collar, which may or may not be accompanied by a buttonhole placket.

SELF COLLAR

On the front, keep a certain number of stitches pending and form the neckband by making decreases on each side, several times, the stitches needed for the size of the garment. Finish each side separately and close the shoulders.

For the back, work as you did for the front except make a shallower neckline.

Sew the shoulders. Then, with four double-pointed needles, pick up the number of stitches around the neck, beginning on one shoulder and picking up the pending stitches in the front and back. Work a few rows in stockinette stitch and bind off the stitches purlwise on the front. Cut the yarn and work it back into the first stitch of the neckband. The band will roll a bit on itself, giving it a fashionable look.

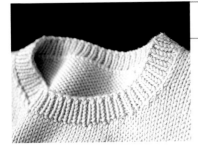

COLLAR FINISHED IN RIB KNIT

Sew the shoulders.

With four double-pointed needles, pick up the necessary number of stitches around the neck, beginning at one of the shoulders.

Pick up the same number of stitches on the two sides of the front and back. Knit the stitches at the center if they have been left pending on a holder, or pick up one stitch per each stitch if they have been bound off.

Knit around using 1/1 or 2/2 rib stitch (you must have a number of stitches divisible by 2 or 4) to the desired height, then bind off all the stitches in ribbing.

COLLAR FINISHED IN A TURTLENECK

Sew the shoulders.

Pick up the stitches with a set of double-pointed needles, then knit around, in 1/1 or 2/2 rib stitch, to the desired height of the collar for 6-1/2" to 9-1/2" (17 to 24 cm).

Bind all the stitches in ribbing.

Fold the collar over.

VARIATION
You can knit a so-called "funnel" neck by finishing the border of the collar at 3" (7 to 8 cm) in height.

COLLAR FINISHED IN A POLO NECK

Sew the shoulders.

Pick up an uneven number of stitches along placket edge (for making buttonholes, see pages 156-157).

Work in 1/1 ribbing for 2-1/2" (6 to 7 cm) or width of placket opening, then bind off all the stitches smoothly in ribbing. Repeat on opposite placket edge.

Overlap ribbed bands (buttonhole side on top) and sew bottom edges to bottom edge of packet opening.

VARIATION

The buttonhole placket opens to the left for men's garments (1) and to the right for women's garments (2).

Be sure to space the buttonholes evenly on the placket for a classic and elegant finish.

V-NECK COLLAR

The v-neck neckband is most often finished with a ribbed border, with decreases in the front center which allow you to accentuate the "v."

With a set of double-pointed needles, pick up the necessary stitches on the back of the collar, then on the side of the front collar down to the tip of the collar. Take up the central stitch left pending and then take up the same number of stitches on the second side of the collar. Based on the type of rib stitch desired (1/1 or 2/2), the number of stitches picked up must be divisible by two or four, without counting the central stitch.

Knit the first row in such a way as to place a purl stitch on the back at the "v" of the collar, and one or two knit stitches on each side of it. On the following row, knit a double decrease at the "v" (see page 43). Repeat this decrease every two (or, less frequently, every four) rows on the three stitches of the "v." Bind off the stitches smoothly in ribbing.

NOTE

All neckbands can also be knitted using two needles. In this case, close only one shoulder, and then assemble the borders very carefully. For a rolled collar or a turtleneck, you must reverse the direction of the sewing at mid-height so that it will not be visible on the outside once the collar is folded over.

Child's Cardigan Sweater with Two Vertical Pockets

THE SWEATER

Size:
2–3 years

Materials:
Anny Blatt Merino Wool
(50 g/125 m balls) 12-1/4 oz (350 g) in the color of your choice
5 1/2" (12 mm) in diameter buttons
Pair each size 1 (2-1/4 m) and 4 (3-1/2 mm) needles

Stitch used:
1/1 rib stitch: K 1, P 1.
Stockinette stitch: K 1 row, P 1 row.

Gauge Swatch:
22 sts and 32 rows = 4" (10 cm) on larger needles.

INSTRUCTIONS

BACK

Cast 95 sts on smaller needles. Work 3" (8 cm) in 1/1 ribbing.

With larger needles, work in stockinette stitch.

At 7-1/2" (19 cm) from beg, bind off 5 sts at beg of next 2 rows, then 3 sts at beg of next 4 rows, then 2 sts at beg of 2 rows. Dec 1 st each side of next RS row.

At 13-1/2" (34 cm) in total length, shape shoulders and neck at the same time. At each shoulder, bind off 6 stitches every other row 3 times; for neck, place center 15 stitches on a holder, and working each side separately, at each neck edge, bind off 4 stitches every other row twice.

LEFT FRONT

For the pocket linings (make 2), cast 15 stitches on larger needles. Work 1-1/2" (4 cm) in stockinette stitch, then leave stitches pending.

Cast 45 stitches on smaller needles and work 3" (8 cm) in 1/1 ribbing. Work in stockinette stitch on larger needles for 1-1/2" (4 cm), then work pocket opening: Knit 19 sts, then continue on the 15 sts of a pocket lining, (34 sts), leaving the rem 26 front sts pending on the left needle. Work 2-1/2" (6.5 cm) on the 34 sts, then on final purl row, bind off the 15 sts of the pocket lining, work the 19 front sts and leaving them pending.

Work 2-1/2" (6.5 cm) on the waiting 26 sts; then leave them pending again.

Now work over all the front sts, working the 19 of the right and the 26 pending, (45 sts).

At 7-1/2" (19 cm) from beg, shape armhole: At arm edge, bind off 5 sts once, then 3 stitches every other row twice, 2 sts once; decrease 1 st every other row once, (31 sts).

At 11-1/2" (29 cm) from beg, shape neck: At center front edge, bind off every other row 5 sts once, 2 sts 3 times; dec 1 st every other row twice, (18 sts).

At 13-1/2" (34 cm) in total length, at arm edge, bind off 6 sts every other row 3 times.

Knit the front right in the same way as you did the front left, except reversing the directions.

SLEEVES

Cast 55 stitches on smaller needles. Work 1-1/2" (4 cm) in 1/1 ribbing.

Work in stockinette stitch on larger needles, increasing 1 stitch every 8 rows 9 times.

At 11" (28 cm) in total length, bind off each side, every 2 rows, 1 times 5 stitches, 4 times 3 stitches, 3 times 2 stitches, 3 times 1 stitch, and then the remaining 21 stitches all at once.

FINISHING TOUCHES

Work the loose yarn ends of the threads into the knitting and then steam-iron the backs of the knitted pieces.

Sew the shoulders and the sides of the sweater, leaving armhole open.

With smaller needles, pick up the 115 stitches along the front right edge. Work 12 rows in 1/1 ribbing. Bind off the stitches in ribbing.

Do the same for the left edge, and on the sixth row form 5 buttonholes of 3 stitches each, the first at 3 stitches from the edge and the rest spaced 23 stitches apart.

With smaller needles, pick up the 101 stitches around the neck edge and front bands, then work 2" (5 cm) in 1/1 ribbing beginning with 1 purl stitch. Bind off the stitches in ribbing.

With smaller needles, pick up the 25 stitches on the front edge of the pocket opening and knit 8 rows in 1/1 ribbing. Bind off the stitches.

Sew the base of the pockets and borders.

Sew the sleeves and attach them.

Sew on the buttons.

4. Armholes

The shape of armholes and sleeves depends on the pattern chosen. We identify several types of armholes: classic, raglan, squared, yoked, or "bat."

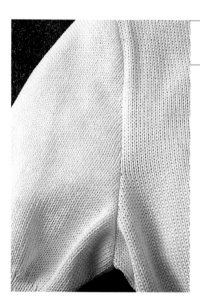

CLASSIC ARMHOLE

The classic armhole is adjusted to the stature and shoulder to receive a classic mounted sleeve, supporting the top of the sleeve; these are also called shaped armholes.

RAGLAN ARMHOLE

The raglan armhole is shaped diagonally from under the arm to the neck. It gives a great deal of ease to the garment because it is deeper than the classic armhole. The decreases on the front, the back, and the sleeves, can be made at two or three stitches from the edge to obtain a decorative effect. In layette knitting, this armhole is often formed by openwork decreases.

SQUARED ARMHOLE

The squared armhole, of the kimono type, is very comfortable for a relaxed garment that is easy for a beginner to make.

The shoulders of a sweater end horizontally, and the top of the sleeve is finished by binding off all the stitches at once.

VARIATIONS

There are other types of armholes, such as an armhole with a yoke or saddle on the shoulder, which is often intended for a "sporty classic" type of garment. The sleeve (called a "hammer sleeve"), is extended by a band the length of the shoulder which is sewn between the front and the back.

The "bat" armhole is a low armhole which makes up an integral part of the garment: the stitches for the sleeves are added to the side edges of the front and back. Front and sleeves (or back and sleeves) making up one single piece, it is critical to make a very large sampler and to compare it with the one indicated on the pattern or the model to be followed.

4. Pockets

Pockets, functional or decorative, add style and comfort to all garments. There are two types of pockets: applied or patch pockets—knitted separately and sewn on the front of the knitting—and split pockets—made up of a border and a pocket lining knitted separately.

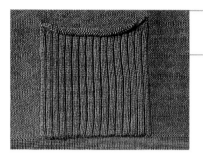

ADVICE

At the start, choose the border of your pocket and cast on a multiple of the number of stitches needed for symmetry. For example, use a multiple of 2 plus 1 for 1/1 ribbing and a multiple of 4 plus 2 for 2/2 ribbing.

APPLIQUED POCKETS

The patch pocket is the easiest to make. It is knitted separately, and you can use whatever stitch you like provided it corresponds with the style of the rest of the knitting. It is then sewn very carefully to the garment, following precisely the stitches and rows, both its own and those of the knitting.

When the pockets are knitted in stockinette stitch, it is preferable to finish them with a border. Those made in garter stitch or seed stitch, for example, do not necessarily need a border.

It is preferable to mark the placing of the pocket on the fronts with a basting thread on a contrasting color. The stitches needed for its completion can also be picked up directly from the knitting.

Knit the pocket in a fancy stitch or in stockinette stitch until you have obtained the desired height, then bind off the stitches. You could also, with the help of thin needles, knit a border in 1/1 or 2/2 rib stitch, respecting the symmetry of the stitch.

INSET POCKETS

Inset pockets are most often placed at one-third of the width of the front from the side seam. The edge of the pocket may finish in a self edge or it can also be integrated into the knitting or picked up afterwards.

The lining of the pocket is knitted separately. It is practical to prepare this in advance: it can thus be integrated immediately when the time comes.

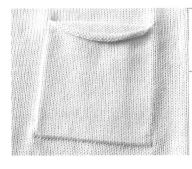

HORIZONTAL INSET POCKETS WITH SELF EDGE

This split pocket is the easiest to make because it finishes in a simple bind off of stitches—a self edge—made in reverse stockinette on stockinette stitch or in stockinette on reverse stockinette stitch. In this way, the border rolls on itself and presents a pretty effect.

Knit the front of the garment up to the pocket opening, then bind off the number of stitches corresponding to the width of the pocket, purlwise on the front or knitwise on the back, and continue to the end of the knitting. Work the pocket lining separately in the same width as the opening, plus 1 selvage stitch on each side. (Selvage sts will be bound off on the last row.) On the next row, work to the pocket opening, work the stitches of the lining with the knit side (RS) facing the purl side (WS) of the front and finish the row.

Continue over all the stitches.

IMPORTANT

You must always mark the placement of the pocket with a basting thread in a contrasting color to clearly visualize its place on the garment.

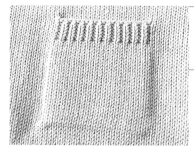

HORIZONTAL INSET POCKETS WITH A PICKED UP RIBBED BORDER

Determine the placement and the width of the pocket. Then knit the lining separately, adding 1 selvage stitch to each side. Bind off the selvage stitches on the last knitted row and keep the other stitches pending.

Knit the front up to the pocket opening, then knit the lining stitches, keep pending the same number of stitches as those of the lining on a stitch holder and finish the row. Continue the work over all the stitches.

ADVICE

When the knitting is done in a fancy stitch, it is preferable to begin the pocket lining in stockinette (to prevent too much thickness) and to finish the last 1" (3 cm) in the fancy stitch. The aesthetic appearance is thus guaranteed when you look inside the pocket.

VARIATION

You can also make horizontal inset pockets with an integrated border: knit the front of the garment just to the pocket opening, subtracting the height of the border 1" (2.5–3 cm), then define its size respecting the symmetry of the stitch for the border.

Continue the work over all the stitches, knitting the border at the same time. Once the height is obtained, bind off the border stitches and finish the row.

Knit the lining of the pocket separately by casting on the same number of stitches as that of the border plus 1 selvage stitch on each side. Once you have knitted to the desired height, about 5" to 6" (12–15 cm), bind off the selvage stitches.

Pick up the stitches on the front and knit, replacing the cast off stitches with those of the pocket lining. Continue to work on all the stitches.

Sew the bottom of the pocket with a slip stitch on the three sides.

VERTICAL INSET POCKETS WITH A BORDER OF PICKED UP STITCHES

Knit until you reach the pocket opening and cast on the same number of stitches on the pocket lining (leave the stitches on the left pending). Continue over all these stitches until you have obtained the desired height of the pocket, then knit the final row binding off those of the lining and leaving the remaining stitches pending.

Work the same height on the left stitches, before leaving them pending.

Then pick up the right stitches, then those on the left, and finish the work over all the stitches.

Once the piece is finished, pick up the stitches for the border on the edge of the split, guarding the symmetry of the stitch, and work the border for 1" (2.5–3 cm). Sew the sides of the border and the lining of the pocket.

VARIATION NUMBER 1

You can also make vertical split pockets with an integrated border: cast on the stitches of the lining of the pocket and knit the latter if necessary over 1" or a few centimeters, then leave the stitches pending.

Determine the placement of the pocket, including the border, on the work. Knit the stitches up to this point, and then knit those of the lining (leave the left stitches pending), just until you reach the desired height of the pocket, about 5" to 6" (12–15 cm). Work the last row and bind off the stitches of the lining and leave the remaining stitches pending.

Take up the stitches pending on the left and knit them, forming at the same time the border on the first stitches. Once you have reached the height, leave the stitches pending.

Take up the stitches on the right, then those on the left, and continue over all the stitches in the stitch used for the project.

Knit the right pocket to correspond.

VARIATION NUMBER 2

Split pockets can also be presented on an angle in certain patterns. They are made using a set of determined dimensions. The borders may be knitted at the same time as the front, or sewn into the work. This work, which is delicate, gives a very haute couture look to classic patterns.

FINISHING POCKETS

Picked up borders on pending stitches can be single or double; the choice is made depending on the function and the style of the garment.

SINGLE BORDERS

These are, most often, made in rib stitches, respecting the symmetry of the stitch.

Take thinner needles (one size smaller) than the ones used for the rest of the work and pick up the stitches left pending.

Knit the border over 1" (2.5 to 3 cm), then bind off all the stitches smoothly.

Sew the selvages of the border onto the garment.

These borders can also be made in a fancy stitch, which will allow you to extend the basic knitting stitch, for example, ribs and small cables.

DOUBLE BORDERS

These borders, which give a very clean and more classic appearance to the finished pocket, are made in stockinette stitch.

With thinner needles (one size smaller) than the ones used for the rest of the work, pick up the stitches left pending.

Work 1" (2.5 to 3 cm) in stockinette stitch, then a purl row on the knit row (foldline) and work to the same height once more in stockinette stitch.

Bind off the stitches.

Fold this border with WS together and sew the edge and the sides.

Child's Pullover Sweater with Horizontal Pockets

THE SWEATER

Size:
2–3 years

Materials:
Anny Blatt Merino Wool (50g/125m balls), 10-1/2 oz (300 g) in the color of your choice
Pair each sizes 3 (3-1/4 mm) and 4 (3-1/2 mm) needles

Stitch used:
1/1 rib stitch: K 1, P 1.
Stockinette stitch: K 1 row, P 1 row.

Gauge Swatch:
22 sts and 32 rows = 4" (10 cm) on larger needles

INSTRUCTIONS

BACK

Cast 88 stitches on smaller needles and work 1-1/2" (4 cm) in 1/1 ribbing.

With larger needles, work in stockinette stitch.

At 14-1/2" (37 cm) in total length, bind off 9 stitches at beg of next 6 rows for the shoulders. Then bind off the 34 remaining stitches for neck.

FRONT

For the pocket linings, cast 19 stitches on larger needles. Work 3" (8 cm) in stockinette stitch, then leave the stitches pending.

Cast 88 stitches on smaller needles and work 1-1/2" (4 cm) in 1/1 ribbing. Work in stockinette stitch on larger needles.

At 5-1/2" (14 cm) from beg, knit 13 sts, leaving the next 19 sts of the front pending on a holder, knit the 19 sts of one pocket lining; knit the center 24 sts of front, leaving the next 19 sts of the front pending, knit 19 sts of the other pocket lining, knit the remaining 13 sts. Continue in stockinette stitch on these 88 stitches.

At 12-1/4" (31 cm) from beg, bind the center 10 sts for neck, and working each side separately, at each neck edge, bind off every other row, 3 sts once, 2 sts 3 times; dec 1 st every other row 3 times. Work even on 27 sts on each side.

At 14-1/2" (37 cm) in total length, at each shoulder, bind off 9 stitches every other row 3 times.

SLEEVES

Cast 57 stitches on smaller needles and work 3" (8 cm) in 1/1 ribbing. Work in stockinette stitch with larger needles, increasing 3 stitches evenly across first row. Then increase 1 stitch at each side every 8 rows 8 times. Work even on 76 stitches.

At 11-3/4" (30 cm) in total length, smoothly bind off the remaining sts.

FINISHING TOUCHES

Work the loose yarn ends into the knitting and then steam-iron the backs of the knitted pieces.

With smaller needles, pick up the 19 pending stitches for the pocket openings and work 3/4" (2 cm) in 1/1 ribbing. Bind off the stitches in ribbing.

Sew the left shoulder. With smaller needles, pick up 34 stitches on the back neck, 27 stitches on the front side, 12 stitches at the center front, and 27 stitches on the other front side. Knit 3/4" (2 cm) in 1/1 ribbing. Smoothly bind off the stitches in ribbing.

Make side edges of front and back 6-3/4" (17 cm) below shoulder seams. Attach top of sleeve between markers. Then seam sleeves and side edges.

Sew the bottom and side edges of pockets in place. Sew side edges of pocket ribbing in place.

Women's Pullover
with Turtleneck and Appliqued Pocket

THE PULLOVER

Size:
Large

Materials:
Bouton d'Or Superwash (50g/155m balls) 25 oz (700 g) in the color of your choice
Pair each of sizes 0 (2 cm), 3 (3-1/4 cm) and 6 (4 cm) needles

Stitch used:
2/2 rib stitch: K 2 sts, P 2 sts.
Reverse stockinette stitch: P I row, K I row.

Gauge Swatch:
27 sts and 36 rows = 4" (10 cm) on largest needles

INSTRUCTIONS

BACK
Cast 162 stitches on medium needles. Work 10 rows in stockinette stitch, then knit 1 row with largest needles and then 10 more rows with medium needles.

Work in reverse stockinette stitch with medium needles.

At 23" (58 cm) from beg, bind off center 36 stitches for neck. Work each side separately: At each neck edge, bind off 4 sts every other row twice.

At 23-3/4" (60 cm) in total length, bind off the remaining 55 stitches on each side for the shoulders.

FRONT
Begin as you did for the back.

At 20-3/4" (53 cm) from beg, bind off the center 26 stitches for the neck. Work each side separately, and at each neck edge, bind off every other row 5 stitches once, 3 stitches once, 2 stitches once; dec 1 st every other row 3 times, (55 sts on each side).

At 23-3/4" (60 cm) in total length, bind off the remaining 55 stitches for each shoulder.

SLEEVES
Cast 84 stitches on medium needles and work the first 21 rows as you did for the front and back. Work in reverse stockinette stitch, increasing 1 st each side every 6 rows 23 times, (130 sts).

At 18" (46 cm) in total length, bind off all stitches.

POCKET
Cast 42 stitches on medium needles. Work 6-1/4" (16 cm) in 2/2 ribbing, then 3/4" (2 cm) in stockinette stitch. Bind off the stitches smoothly, knitting them on the purl side of the work.

NOTE

This collar may be finished with a set of four dpn needles or a dpn circular needle in smallest size. In this case, knit around in 2/2 ribbing for 3" (8 cm); the number of stitches picked up must be divisible by 4.

FINISHING TOUCHES

Work the loose yarn ends into the knitting and then steam-iron the backs of the knitted pieces.

Seam the left shoulder. With medium needles, pick up 44 sts along back neck then 16 stitches on the front side, 26 stitches in the center front and 16 stitches on the other front side, (94 sts). Work 3" (8 cm) 2/2 ribbing and then 3/4" (2 cm) in stockinette stitch. Bind off the stitches smoothly, knitting them on a purl row.

Seam the other shoulder and the edge of the collar.

Mark side edges of front and back 9-1/2" (24 cm) below shoulder seam. Attach sleeve tops between markers on each side. Seam sleeves and the sides of the sweater.

Sew the pocket to the front.

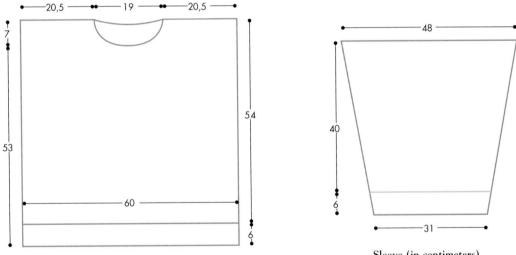

Front and back (in centimeters)

Sleeve (in centimeters)

A hem constitutes the finish of an edge of knitting and makes it resistant, preventing the stitches from curling if they are worked in stockinette stitch. A hemmed finish replaces a ribbed edge.

A hem is also used to finish the bottom of dresses, sleeves and classic vests.

SEWN HEMS

THE FOLD LINE

To define the edge and to make it fold cleanly, a row is usually worked in reverse stockinette stitch (purl on right side).

This foldline defines the base of the hem.

> **NOTE**
>
> If you don't wish the obvious edge of reverse stockinette stitch, work the hem with a size smaller needle which will make it easier to turn up.

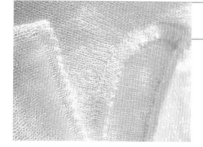

CAT'S TOOTH STITCH

To create a decorative and softer effect (for layette patterns, for example), you can knit a row of picots called "cat's tooth stitch" after a few rows of stockinette stitch.

The number of stitches must always be even.

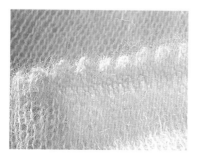

Row 1: K 1 st * yo, K 2 sts tog*, K 1 stitch.
Row 2: P all the sts, including yo.

NOTE

Be sure the tension of the attaching yarn is the same as the knitting.

SEWING THE HEM

The edge of the hems is, in this case, sewn using a simple overcast stitch.

1. Sew, in the regular manner, one stitch of the hem to the corresponding stitch on the reverse side of the knitting.

2. Another method of sewing the hem is to hold the stitches on the needle, then take them up with a tapestry needle to attach them to the piece.

KNITTED HEMS

The hem can also be sewn in reverse stockinette, which give a very pretty finish to the edge of knitting.

Cast the stitches onto needles a size or two smaller than the ones used for the rest of the knitting. Knit the necessary rows for the height of the hem. Work a row of reverse stockinette stitch to mark the lower edge and then knit to the same height again. Hold the stitches on the needle.

1 through 6. Pick up the cast-on stitches. Holding both needles together, work a picked up stitch together with each stitch on the working needle. Continue across the row.

Once all the stitches have been worked, continue knitting with the needles called for on the rest of the piece.

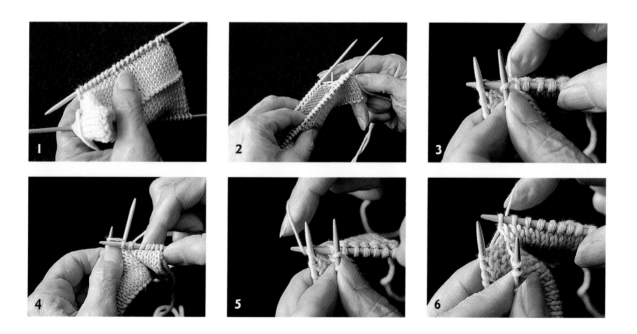

4. Decorations

POMPONS

Making a pompon requires a bit of patience because the wrapping phase takes time, but it is an operation which creates satisfaction when the pompon is finished. This touch enhances berets, scarves, and other garments and can become a fun accessory.

Cut two rounds out of stiff cardboard—their diameter should be equal to that of the size of the finished pompon—then cut a circular center in each of them. The larger it is, the tighter the pompon will be (to make a fluffy pompon with a diameter of 1-1/4" (3.2 cm), for example, the inner circle should be 1/2" (1.3 cm).

1 and 2. Put the two cardboard cutouts one on top of the other, then wind the yarn around the resulting circle until the center circle is completely filled.

3. Slide the tip of a pair of sharp scissors between the two cardboard rounds and cut the yarn around the entire pompon.

4. Slide a sturdy piece of yarn (or use dental floss) between the two cardboard rounds and tie all the strands together. Cut the circles and remove them.

5. Shake the pompon to fluff it out, then trim the strands with the scissors to give the pompon a even, round shape.

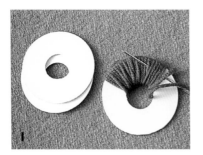

TASSELS

Easy to make, tassels can be placed at the corners of pillows and afghans, and at the ends of scarves. They can be of nearly any length depending on the final use.

1. Wind the yarn around two pieces of thick cardboard one on top of the other, in the desired length, adding about an inch (2.5 cm) to allow for stretching and trimming; wind enough yarn so that the tassel will be full.

2. With a tapestry needle, slide a sturdy yarn under all the strands of yarn at one end, and tie them together.

3. Cut the yarn at the other end of the cardboard, then wind a thread around the tassel about 1/2" (1 cm) from the top, tighten to form the "head" and slip the ends of those two strands inside.

Even the ends of the strands with the scissors.

FRINGE

Fringe is the classic finish on scarves and stoles. It can also finish the bottom of a sweater or a poncho.

1 and 2. Cut two pieces of cardboard about 1 inch (2.5 cm) longer than you would like your fringe, and wind the yarn around the cardboard. Cut the yarn at the lower edge, between the cardboards, to make the strands.

3 to 5. Insert a crochet hook, of a size appropriate to the weight of the yarn, through the stitch of the work from the back to the front, beginning at one edge. Loop the number of strands called for in the pattern, or as you desire, around the hook and pull loop through the piece. Pass the ends of the strands through the loop and pull tight.

6. Place a fringe every three or four stitches, then shake them out to relax them and even the ends with the scissors.

TRIVIA

The fringe at the hem of pants worn by Native Americans erased all traces of their steps so that they could not be followed by enemies.

CORDS

"To lay up a cable," a sailor's expression, finds its equivalent in the knitting world with "to make a cord."

You make a cord in order to tighten pieces of knitting, to draw in the waist of a sweater (you pass the cord through holes made for this purpose) or to decorate the top of a hat with a pompon or a tassel, which balances the piece. The cord also works well for bags and totes.

To estimate the length of the yarn to cut, multiply the length of the finished cord by four and add about a quarter more to this measurement.

I and 2. Cut the yarn, then fold it in two and knot the ends together. Attach one end to a fixed point, such as a doorknob, then insert a pencil between the knot and rotate the pencil to twist the yarn until you cannot twist anymore. Take hold of the twisted strands halfway down. Release the tension and they will twist over on one another. Smooth them with your fingers to even out the twists. Knot both ends. You can make a thicker cord working with more strands of yarn.

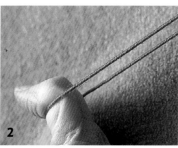

Neck Scarves with Four Pompons

THE COLLARS

Size:
7"x 40" (18 x 100 cm)

Materials:
1-3/4 oz (50 grams) lightweight angora or mohair in the colors of your choice
Contrasting scraps for the pompons
Pair size 4 (3.5 mm) needles
Tapestry needle

Stitches used:
Stockinette stitch: K 1 row, P 1 row.
Reverse stockinette stitch: P 1 row, K 1 row.

Gauge Swatch:
22 sts and 32 rows = 4" (10cm)

INSTRUCTIONS

Cast on 40 sts and K 5 sts in rev St st, 30 stitches in St st, and then 5 sts in rev St st.

Work in pat as established for 40" (100 cm). Bind off.

At 40" (100 cm) in total length, bind off the stitches.

FINISHING TOUCHES

Make four pompons 1" (2.5 cm) in diameter and attach them to the corners of the scarf.

5

Assembly and Care

Assembly

To block pieces before assembly, place the pieces on a flat surface on top of two or three terry cloth towels. Pin pieces to the proper dimensions, having the pins about 1" (2.5 cm) apart and on a slight angle with the point angled toward the center of the piece.

Place a damp cloth over the pieces. Using the proper setting for the fiber of the pieces, pass an iron lightly over them. Put no pressure on the iron; it is the heat, not the weight, that sets the size. Remove the cloth and allow the pieces to dry thoroughly. Remove pins and assemble.

Always check your labels since not all yarns require blocking.

SEWING WITH A BACKSTITCH

The two pieces are placed with right sides together, and the stitching is done on the reverse side of the work.

1. For a flat seam such as the shoulder, use a tapestry needle and yarn that coordinates with the color of the knitting. Here, we used a contrasting color yarn to highlight the procedure.

2. Insert the needle under the knitting and bring it back out on top, two stitches ahead.

3. Insert the needle back in the first stitch and bring it up, according to the thickness of the work, in the next stitch or two stitches ahead.

At the end of the work, firmly fasten off the thread.

For sleeves, mark the center of the sleeve cap and line it up with the shoulder seam. With right sides together, sew them in place easing the stitches at the top of the cap.

SEWING TOGETHER TWO PARTS WORKED IN DIFFERENT DIRECTIONS

TIPS

Before beginning to join the sleeve to the body, count the number of stitches and the number of rows that you have to be joined. If the amounts are not equal add or subtract as necessary.

To attach the sleeve to the body, insert the needle through the two parts of each stitch on the sleeve and between the corresponding two stitches of the edge of the body, passing under the horizontal bar which separates the rows.

INVISIBLE STITCH TO STITCH SEWING

Sewing side seams is done stitch to stitch to be invisible.

The sewing is done on the right side of the work, placing the two pieces flat, side by side. Use the same yarn used in the work and a tapestry needle. Insert the needle into the middle of the edge stitch. Pass it through the bar and then into the matching bar of the other piece. Pull tight. We've left the seam open and used contrasting color yarn so you can see how it is done.

SEWING BUTTONS

NOTE

Sew all buttons horizontally if they have two holes and vertically if they have four holes.

Buttons are sewn with silk or mercerized cotton thread in a color which matches the work and/or the buttons as you choose.

Use a pointed sewing needle. Make three or four passes through the holes in the button keeping the thread a bit loose. After the last pass, wrap the thread around the stitches, between the button and the knitted piece and fasten off.

GRAFTING, OR INVISIBLE HORIZONTAL JOINING

Grafting is used to join two pieces of knitting in order to give the appearance of one continuous knit whose stitches have never been separated. This technique is often used to assemble the stitches of shoulders; it is ideal to finish mittens or socks, because the result offers the advantage of greater comfort, the stitches being assembled or "grafted" invisibly and without a thick seam.

If you are working without a knitting needle, it is necessary to block the stitches by gently pressing them with a damp cloth, to make sure they do not come undone. However, to make the yarn pass more smoothly through the stitches, it is preferable to place them on a needle.

1. Place the two parts on a flat surface directly next to each other. Use a tapestry needle and thread a piece of yarn four times longer than the length of the pieces to be joined. Work from right to left or if you are left-handed from left to right.

2. Insert the needle into the first stitch of the lower piece, from back to front, and then in the first stitch of the upper piece from front to back, and into the next stitch of the upper piece from back to front. Then insert the needle again into the first stitch of the lower piece, from front to back and into the next stitch from back to front.

Insert the needle into the second stitch of the upper piece from front to back, then into the third stitch from back to front.

Continue in this manner until the joining of the two pieces is complete and invisible. If necessary, even out the tension of the yarn, stitch by stitch, starting where you began the work.

TIP

A final light blocking on the seams, neckbands, armholes, edges and pockets will give a final professional touch to your knitting.

NOTE

The shoulder seams may be joined by grafting if you desire and if the shoulder is planned to be bound off all at once. In this case do not bind off, instead slip the stitches to a holder.

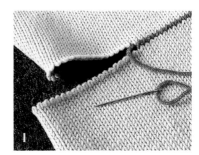

Practical Tips and Care

Taking care of your handmade work is up to you. You may choose to hand-wash items rather than machine wash, even though manufacturer's recommendations allow for such. Once dry, the piece should be folded to be stored. Never hang hand knitted pieces.

RECYCLING PREVIOUSLY USED YARN

Undo the seams. Separating each ball or skein, wind the yarn around a straight chair back forming a hank. Tie hank in two or three places with a figure-eight knot. Soak in lukewarm water to relax the fibers. Do not wring. Hang each hank over a wire hanger and let dry over a bathtub or other waterproof container. The weight of the water will pull the kinks out. When dry, wind into balls.

HAND WASHING

To hand wash, use a detergent for delicate fabrics or a baby shampoo. Dilute the cleanser in lukewarm water. Turn the piece inside out and place in. Squeeze lightly without stretching it (gently rub soiled areas).

Rinse several times in fresh water of the same temperature, adding a bit of fabric softener in the final rinse. Dry flat on a terry towel.

MACHINE WASHING

For machine washing, make sure that your machine has a setting for delicate fabrics, and carefully follow the care directions on the yarn label. Again, turn the piece inside out.

DRYING

TIP

A drop of vinegar in the final rinse will remove any lingering cleaner and revitalize the colors. Once the piece is dry, the piece should be folded and placed in a drawer with an anti-moth agent (such as mothballs), which will guarantee your piece long life.

For drying, press the piece without twisting to remove as much water as possible, and place it flat on an terrycloth towel. Cover it with a second towel, roll up, and press again, then unroll it and lay the piece out on a dry towel or a screen-type flat rack, making sure it has been shaped to size.

Always dry indoors away from any source of heat. Always dry your knitting flat.

BLOCKING

NOTE

The damp cloth used in blocking is a piece of cotton or linen, which you dampen and place on the woolen garment before lightly applying the iron to them.

Before blocking, read the yarn band for advice. Some yarns may not need blocking.

Blocking is the step which comes before assembling the different parts of the piece. It is done using a damp cloth such as a dish towel. Blocking is done on the back of the work. Use rustproof pins to secure the edges, adjusting the tensions to get the exact dimensions desired.

A final blocking after joining the pieces will flatten the seams and give a professional look to the garment, which you have pampered with love from the very beginning.

6

Appendix

Visual Index of Stitches and Techniques

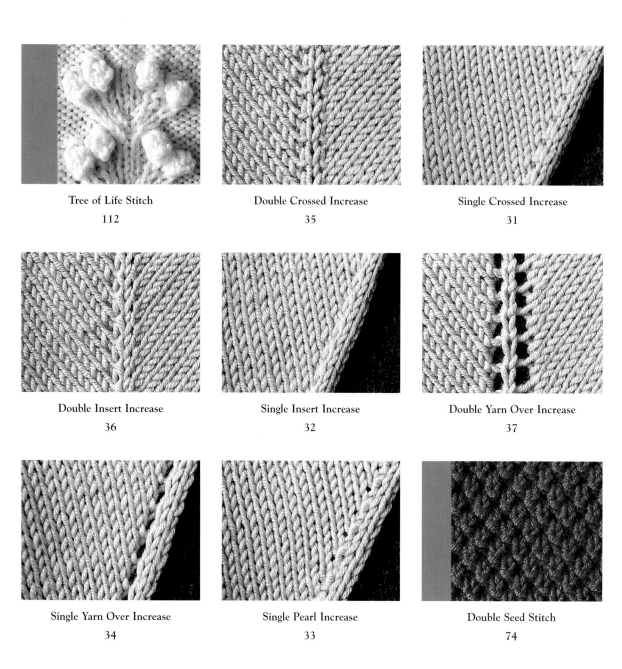

Tree of Life Stitch
112

Double Crossed Increase
35

Single Crossed Increase
31

Double Insert Increase
36

Single Insert Increase
32

Double Yarn Over Increase
37

Single Yarn Over Increase
34

Single Pearl Increase
33

Double Seed Stitch
74

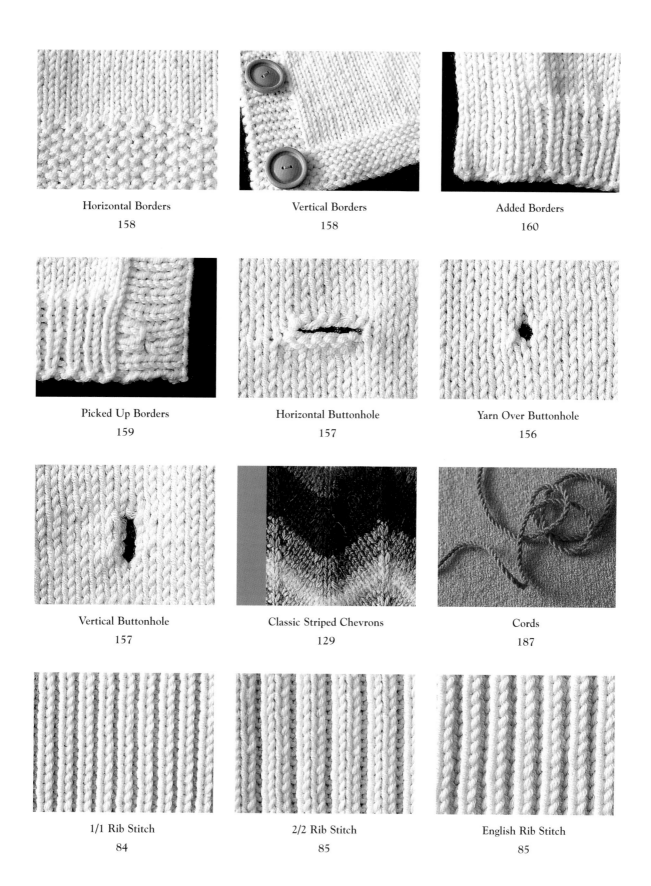

Horizontal Borders
158

Vertical Borders
158

Added Borders
160

Picked Up Borders
159

Horizontal Buttonhole
157

Yarn Over Buttonhole
156

Vertical Buttonhole
157

Classic Striped Chevrons
129

Cords
187

1/1 Rib Stitch
84

2/2 Rib Stitch
85

English Rib Stitch
85

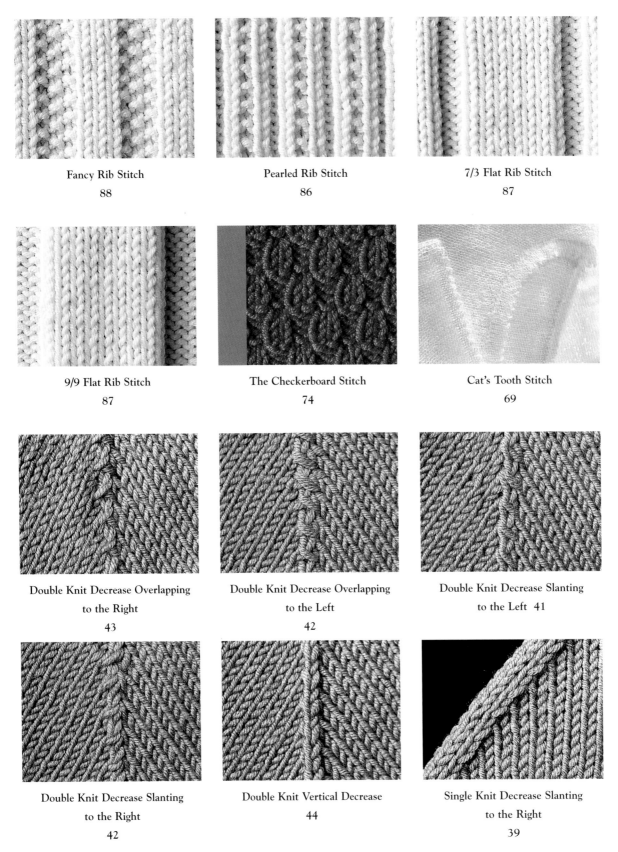

Fancy Rib Stitch
88

Pearled Rib Stitch
86

7/3 Flat Rib Stitch
87

9/9 Flat Rib Stitch
87

The Checkerboard Stitch
74

Cat's Tooth Stitch
69

Double Knit Decrease Overlapping
to the Right
43

Double Knit Decrease Overlapping
to the Left
42

Double Knit Decrease Slanting
to the Left 41

Double Knit Decrease Slanting
to the Right
42

Double Knit Vertical Decrease
44

Single Knit Decrease Slanting
to the Right
39

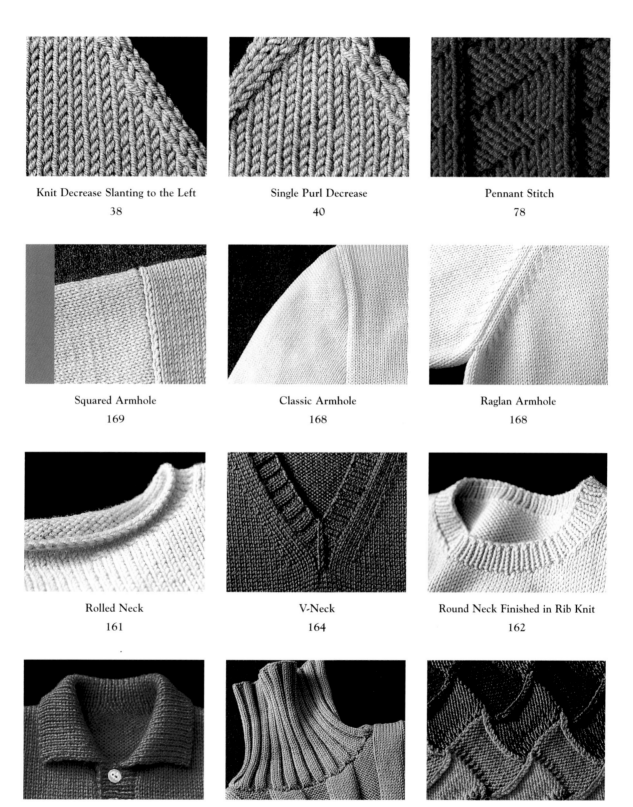

Knit Decrease Slanting to the Left
38

Single Purl Decrease
40

Pennant Stitch
78

Squared Armhole
169

Classic Armhole
168

Raglan Armhole
168

Rolled Neck
161

V-Neck
164

Round Neck Finished in Rib Knit
162

Round Neck with in a Polo Collar
163

Round Neck with a Turtleneck
162

Entrelac or Interlace
136

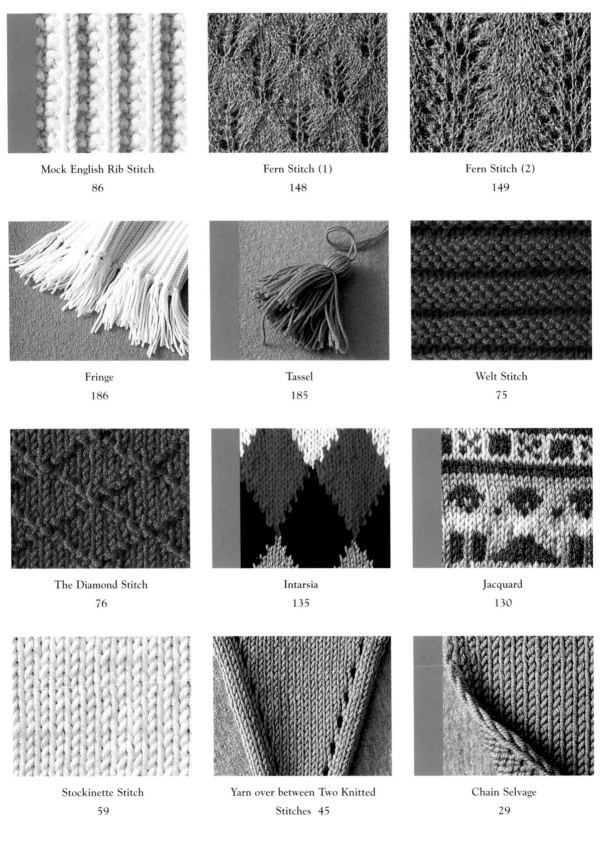

Mock English Rib Stitch
86

Fern Stitch (1)
148

Fern Stitch (2)
149

Fringe
186

Tassel
185

Welt Stitch
75

The Diamond Stitch
76

Intarsia
135

Jacquard
130

Stockinette Stitch
59

Yarn over between Two Knitted
Stitches 45

Chain Selvage
29

Seam Selvage
29

Double Pearl Selvage
30

Single Pearl Selvage
30

Garter Stitch Selvage
30

Cabled Diamonds with a
Seed Stitch Center
114

Madeira Stitch
149

Cable Stitches Without a
Cable Needle
118

Twisted Stitches
122

Bobbles
120

Garter Stitch
58

Cat's Eye Stitch
146

Cables
104

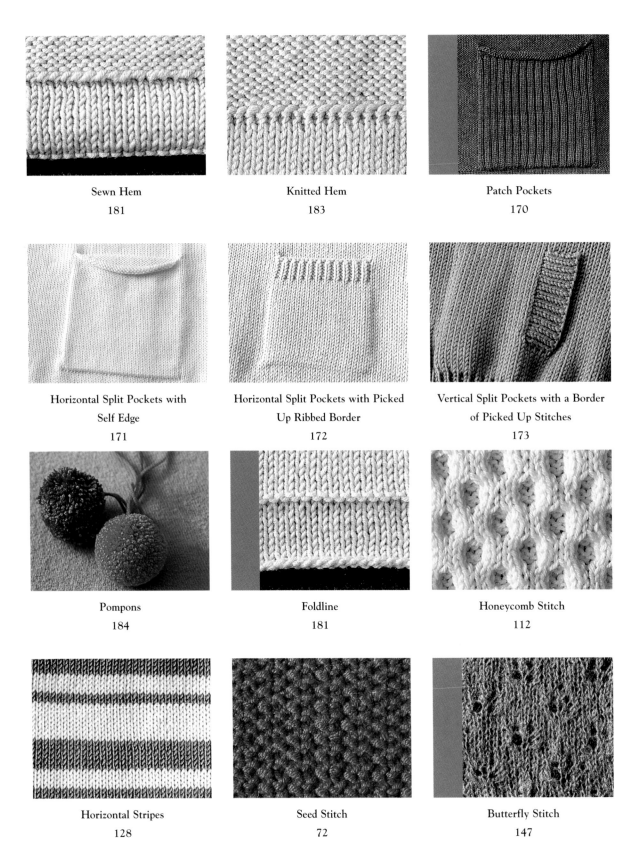

Sewn Hem
181

Knitted Hem
183

Patch Pockets
170

Horizontal Split Pockets with
Self Edge
171

Horizontal Split Pockets with Picked
Up Ribbed Border
172

Vertical Split Pockets with a Border
of Picked Up Stitches
173

Pompons
184

Foldline
181

Honeycomb Stitch
112

Horizontal Stripes
128

Seed Stitch
72

Butterfly Stitch
147

Slip, Knit and Pass Decrease
46

English Bind Off
48

Belgian Bind Off on Stockinette Stitch
49

Belgian Bind Off on Garter Stitch
49

Regular Bind Off
47

Corded Cable Stitch
101

Open Front Cables
103

Double Cable
102

Woven Cable
102

Cable on a Background of Seed Stitch
103

Basic Cable
100

Cable and Rib Pattern
100

Braided Cable
101

Trinity Stitch
111

Zigzag Stitch
77

Clean graph to use to compose your own jacquard motifs and fancy patterns

Table of Projects

Baby Blanket and Bootees

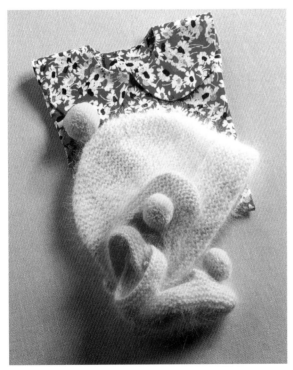

Fuzzy Cap and Bootees with Pompons

Child's Sweater in the Garter and Stockinette Stitches

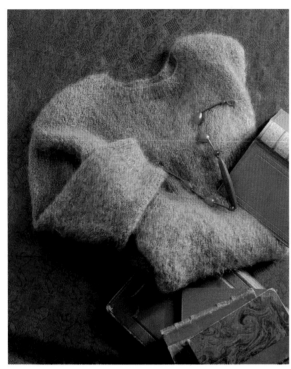

Tunic
66

Kid Mohair Sweater with Cat's Tooth Stitch Sleeves
69

Two Caps and a Beret
79

Toddler's Tricolor Cardigan
82

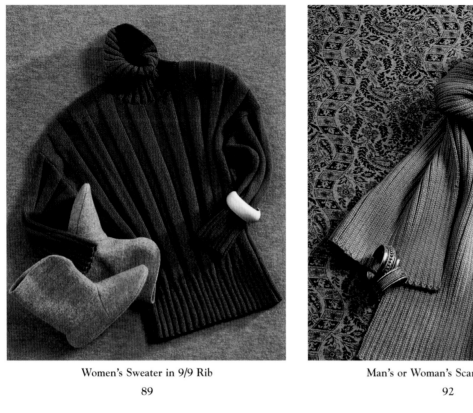

Women's Sweater in 9/9 Rib
89

Man's or Woman's Scarf in 2/2 Rib
92

Scarf or Stole in Fancy Rib
94

Small Angora Lap Blanket in English Rib
96

Toddler's Cable Sweater
105

Natural Wool Sweater in Wave Stitch
108

Men's Sailor Sweater
123

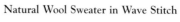

Dandy Wrist Muffs
126

Jacquard Knee-Socks and Scarf

140

Child's Little Doggy Sweater

143

Airy Baby Blankets and Stole in Kid Mohair

150

Fashion Scarf in Kid Mohair

152

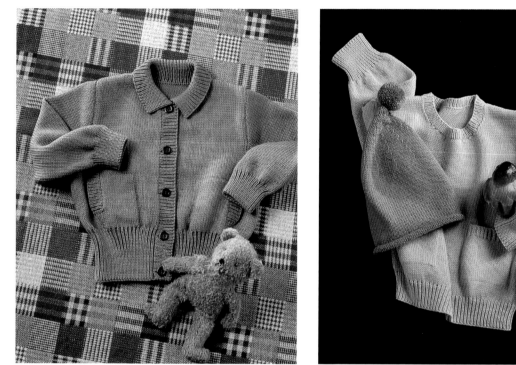

Child's Cardigan Sweater with Two Vertical Pockets

165

Child's Pullover Sweater with Horizontal Pockets

175

Women's Pullover with Turtleneck and Patch Pocket

178

Neck Scarves with Four Pompons

188

Index

Techniques & Abbreviations

KNITTING NEEDLES

US	Metric	UK	US	Metric	UK
0	2 mm	14	10	6 mm	4
1	2.25 mm	13	10-1/2	6.5 mm	3
2	2.5 mm			7 mm	2
	2.75 mm	12		7.5 mm	1
3	3 mm		11	8 mm	0
	3.25 mm	10	13	9 mm	00
4	3.5 mm		15	10 mm	000
5	3.75 mm	9	17	12.75 mm	
6	4 mm	8	19	16 mm	
7	4.5 mm	7	35	19 mm	
8	5 mm	6	50	25.5 mm	
9	5.5 mm	5			

GENERAL YARNS GAUGES

Sts per 4"/10cm	Weight
29–32 sts	fine
25–28 sts	light
21–24 sts	medium
17–20 sts	medium-heavy
13–16 sts	bulky
9–12 sts	extra-bulky

KNITTING ABBREVIATIONS

approx	approximately
beg	beginning
CC	contrasting color
ch	chain
cm	centimeter(s)
cn	cable needle
cont	continu(e)(ing)
dec	decreas(e)(ing)
dpn	double pointed needle(s)
foll	follow(s)(ing)
g	gram(s)
inc	increas(e)(ing)

k	knit
LH	Lefthand
lp(s)	loop(s)
m	meter(s)
mm	millimeter(s)
MC	main color
MI	make one (see glossary)
MI p-st	make one purl stitch (see glossary)
oz	ounce(s)
p	purl
pat(s)	pattern(s)
pm	place marker
psso	pass slip stitch(es) over
rem	remain(s)(ing)
rep	repeat
RH	righthand
RS	right side(s)
rnd(s)	round(s)
SKP	slip 1, knit 1, pass slip stitch over, 1 stitch has been decreased

SK2P	slip 1, knit 2 together, pass slip stitch ver the knit 2 together, 2 stitches have been decreased.
sl s	lip
sl st	slip stitch (see glossary)
ssk	slip, slip knit (see glossary)
sssk	slip, slip, slip, knit (see glossary)
st(s)	stitch(es)
tbl	through back loop(s)
tog	together
WS	wrong side(s)
wyib	with yarn in back
wyif	with yarn in front yard(s)
yd	yard(s)
yo	yarn over needle (UK: see glossary)
*	repeat directions following * as many times as indicated
[]	repeat direction inside brackets as many times as indicated

Glossary

bind off or cast off

Used to finish an edge or segment. Lift the first stitch over the second, the second over the third, etc. (UK: cast off).

bind off in ribbing

Work in ribbing as you bind off. (Knit the knit stitches, purl the purl stitches) (UK: cast off in ribbing).

3-needle bind off

With the right side of the two pieces facing and the needles parallel, insert a third needle into the first stitch on each needle and knit them together. Knit the next two stitches the same way. Slip the first stitch on the third needle over the second stitch and off the needle. Repeat for 3-needle bind-off.

cast on

A foundation row of stitches placed upon the needle in order to begin knitting.

decrease

Reduce the stitches in a row by knitting 2 together. Most often done near the beginning and the end of the row.

increase

Add stitches in a row (i.e., knit in front and back of stitch).

knitwise

Insert the needle into the stitch as if you were going to knit it.

make one

With the needle tip, lift the strand between last stitch knit and next stitch onto the lefthand needle and knit into back of it. One knit stitch has been added.

make one p-st

With the needle tip, lift the strand between last stitch worked and next stitch on the lefthand needle and purl it. One purl stitch has been added.

no stitch

On some charts, "no stitch" is indicated with shaded spaces where stitches have been decreased or not yet made. In such cases, work the stitches of the chart, skipping over the "no stitch" spaces.

place markers

Place or attach a loop of contrast yarn or purchased stitch marker as indicated.

pick up and knit (purl)
Knit (or purl) into the loops along an edge.

purlwise
Insert the needle into the stitch as if you were going to purl it.

selvage stitch
Edge stitch that helps make seaming easier.

slip, slip, slip, knit
Slip next 3 stitches knitwise, one at a time, to right-hand needle. Insert tip of lefthand needle into fronts of these stitches from left to right. Knit them together. Two stitches have been decreased.

slip stitch
An unworked stitch made by passing a stitch from the lefthand to the righthand needle, usually as if to purl.

work even
Continue in pattern without increasing or decreasing (UK: work straight).

yarn over
Making a new stitch by wrapping the yarn over the righthand needle (UK: yfwd, yon, yrn).

BASIC STITCH

Garter stitch
Knit every row. Circular knitting: knit one round, then purl one round.

Stockinette stitch
Knit right-side rows and purl wrong-side rows. Circular knitting: knit all rounds (UK: stocking stitch).

Reverse Stockinette stitch
Purl right-side rows and knit wrong-side rows. Circular knitting, purl all rounds (UK: reverse stocking stitch).

Acknowledgments

I would first like to pause to acknowledge my mother and maternal grandmother, who, when I was very young, taught me knitting, card games, writing, and geography, without ever boring me, forcing me, or pestering me: they opened my eyes and my soul to wonderful new worlds.

I would like to thank Éditions Solar, Suyapa and Aurélie; I thank Sabine Dubois, the Pierre de Loye Society for Anny Blatt and Bouton d'Or threads.

I have a deep gratitude for Jean-Charles Vaillant, with whom I have had the immense pleasure of working: our collaboration has been so positive for me. His eye, his perception of things and his critique have been indispensable, and the meetings and photo shoots will always be a fond memory.

Thanks to Bernard, my husband, who has helped me so much as I was writing this book.

Thanks to Mrs. Aubert, Mrs. Lagasse, Mrs. Dullens, Mrs. Dufresnes, Mrs. Musset, Mrs. Whyte and Mrs. Beneston, without whom the patterns in this book would not have been made in time. These women sustained and supported me in my moments of doubt.

A final thought for my dear daughters, Anne and Sybille, whom I thank for listening to me and for their patience with me.

Luce Smits

...les rochelles, l'Irlande, les

...rains et l'océan, le phare et la

...rie. Tweed et chevrons, malt et

...pain gris. L'arbre de vie, les métiers

...et les chaussettes et le petit talon.

...es lamas et l'alpaga, les lapins et

...l'angora et Philippe le forestier. L...

...in, les Flandres et la mer. Toujours

...ugmenter, toujours diminuer, tou...

...répéter. Les écharpes pour l'automne

...es pulls pour l'hiver, le coton pour la pl...

...et les livres à l'infini.